Memories of Houghton Regis

Edited by Sue King

Published October 2011 by
Book Castle Publishing
2a Sycamore Business Park
Copt Hewick
North Yorkshire HG4 5DF

© Sue King, 2011

The right of Sue King to be identified as the author of this work has been assumed by her in accordance with the Copyright, Designs and Patents Act 1988

ISBN 978 1 906632 12 0

Typeset and designed by Tracey Moren, Moren Associates Limited
www.morenassociates.co.uk

Printed in Great Britain by Lonsdale Print Solutions Ltd, Wellingborough.

Cover Picture: Beer barrel rolling race (DG/LM)
Back Cover Picture: Houghton Hall (SK)

Contents

Introduction	vii
Houghton's Hidden History	1
Village Life	11
Houghton's Tradespeople	52
Memories of a Butcher's Boy	66
Journey to the Other Side of the World...	87
Cement Manufacture in Houghton Regis	108
A New Life...	121

* * * *

With the support of Central Bedfordshire Council

* * * *

All proceeds from the sale of this book will be donated to charities within Houghton Regis.

Post War to Pre-development Representation of Shops, Businesses & Landmarks in Houghton Regis Village Centre

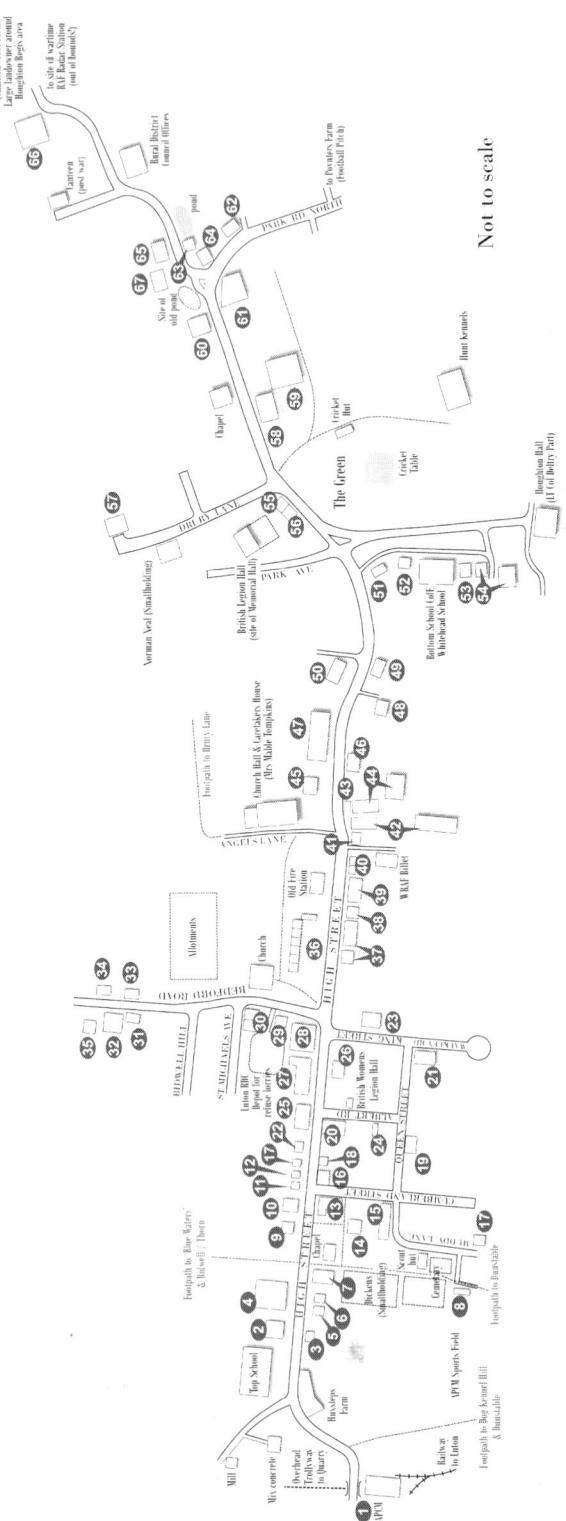

1. APCM - Associated Portland Cement **Manufacturers**
2. Ashdown (Milkman)
3. Bert Higgs (Shoe Mender)
4. Tompkins/Hobbs (Garage)
5. Baughan's (Cycle Shop)
6. Miss Tims (Sweet Shop)
7. Five Bells PH (Mr Mrs Thorpe)
8. Vince Bozier (Healer)
9. Bakery
10. Shaw's (General Store)
11. John Odmans (Newsagent)
12. Jack Brooks (Shoe Shop & Repairs)
13. Jack Tompkins (Butcher. Slaughter House)
   Shop - Various - Opticians
14. Disused Chapel (Furniture. House Fittings)
15. Ben Tompkins (Decorator. Handyman)
16. White Horse Public House
17. Harry Price (Beekeeper) - Hives off Cemetery
   Road (Muddy Lane)
18. Bert East (Greengrocer)
19. Percy Ward (Bakers)
20. Country Side Laundry
21. Henry Bandy (Builder)
22. Cliff Sinfield (Hairdresser)
23. Jack Bishop (Builder)
24. King (General Builder)
25. General Store - then Ken Edwards
   (first self-service Store)
26. Gravestock (General Store / Post Office)
27. Car repairs (was Butchers / Cattle Dealers)
28. Kings Arms Public House
29. Warren (Sweet shop, Café)
30. Robinson (Shoe mender) / Goosey (Builder,
   Estate Agent)
31. D Green (Poultry, Farmer)
32. Old Red Lion
33. H Green (Poultry, Farmer)
34. R Green (Farmer, Milkman)
35. Harris (Farmer)
36. Workhouse Row / Outside Toilets
37. Jones (General Store) became Co-op
38. Birds Bakery
39. Jasper Perry (General Store)
40. Miss Freemans House (Schoolteacher)
   related to Gary Cooper
41. The White House (Captain Smith)
42. Pratts (Butcher & Smallholding)
43. Miss Bussell (Millenary & Handicraft)
44. Timmy Allen Knacker Yard (dog meat & Hunt supplies)
45. House - was Pub (name not known)
46. Tompkins Forge (Metalworker) - then Midland Bank
   first bank in Houghton Regis (Manager Perry
47. Wainwright - Dunstable Mayor)
   Smiths Farmhouse
48. Lillywhites (Nurserymen & Timber Merchants)
49. Tansley (Fish & Chip Shop)
50. The Tythe Barn
51. Gert Smith (Sweet Shop)
52. The Red House (The Allen Family)
53. Headmasters House (Mr Sidney Chaperlin)
54. General Smythe House (Farm & Stables)
55. Houghton Hall Cottages - Butlers Home (Mr Townsend)
56. Mr Frank Buckingham (Music Teacher)
57. Birchleys (Greengrocer, Garden Supplies)
58. The Crown Public House
59. Ben Meachem (Garage & Car Repairs)
60. The Firs (Mr & Mrs Martin)
61. The Chequers Public House
62. Police House (Sgt Fred Montague. Buckle Dee.
   Doug Reece)
63. Dene Hollow (Mr & Mrs Carruthers)
64. Chantry Farm House
65. Jack Blow (Farmer)
66. Catlin (Pig Farmer. General Dealer)
67. George Aye (Cabinet Maker)

v

Individual contributions in alphabetical order:

William Aries
June Baldock (nee Sinfield)
Mrs Pauline Joy Baynton
Victor & Mary Bird
Mrs & Mrs Burnage
Mrs P Cameron
Irene Carpenter
Gloria Carruthers
Chris Charman
Mr & Mrs Cherry
Gwyneth Clarke
Mr D J Dickens
Mrs Dove
Mr L R Dyer
Janice Enright (nee Dunn)
Frances Fisher
Ruth Francis-Foster (nee Baldock)
Pat Gidley
Richard Goosey
Betty Grayson
Richard Hagen
Richard Hall
Mike Holwill
Renee S Hyde (nee Ward)
Alan A Johns
Lafarge Cement UK plc – David Simms and Dr Chris Downs
Beryl Lovegrove
Pat Lovering
Mrs Beryl Morton
Catherine Phillips
Peter Pratt

Mr A J Reid
Mr D R Riley
Terry Sharp
Mr M Sturnum
Mr & Mrs P Todd
Geoffrey Tompkins
Keith & Val Wallis
Michael Wiles
Richard Woollison

I would also like to thank the following people for allowing me to use their photographs:

County Record Office, Bedford (CRO)
Gloria Curruthers (GC)
Mr D J Dickens (DJD)
Mrs Dove (RD)
Dunstable Gazette (DG)
David Fookes (DF)
Richard Goosey (RG)
Richard Hagen (RHA)
Richard Hall (RH)
Renee S Hyde (nee Ward) (RSH)
Pat Lovering (PL)
Luton Museum (LM)
Peter Pratt (PP)
Dudley Smy (DS)
Geoffrey Tompkins (GT)
Michael Wiles (MW)
Sue King (SK)

Introduction

Memories of Houghton Regis is a collection of reminiscences and stories from people who were either born in Houghton Regis, or who decided to move to the town and have made it their home. It has been a pleasure to meet so many wonderful people, and I would like to thank everyone who has very kindly given me their recollections and photographs to use in this book. I would especially like to thank Pat Lovering for her superb help and support.

The reminiscences cover a time period from around the early 1940s to the present day. It has not been possible to include every story, and some editing has been required to allow as many stories to be included as possible. Houghton Regis has changed considerably in recent history, and some versions of past events may not tally with those of others. But memories change with time and people will recall events in a myriad of different ways.

*****

Surrounded by beautiful countryside, Houghton Regis has attracted thousands of people to live and work within its boundaries over many years.

Travel back to the 1940s and you would have discovered an attractive Bedfordshire village, typical of its time, with a 15th century church, village pond, local farms, village green, alms-houses and a great variety of thriving shops, businesses and character cottages lining the main High Street. Tithe Farm, together with its Barn, thought to have been built between 1396 & 1401 by Abbot John Moore, nestled just to the rear of the High Street, next to the very substantial Tithe Farm House, with its distinctive four chimneys.

A farming village for centuries, hundreds of men earned their living working on the land, while straw plaiting and hat making was a major occupation for many women and children.

As these industries began to decline, the opening of two railway lines, to Leighton Buzzard in 1848 and to Luton in 1858, provided much-needed jobs for people in the area. Two railway stations were established in the village – these no longer exist, but before the introduction of boundary changes, they were based in Church Street, and in High Street North, Upper Houghton. Other industries came to Houghton Regis, including Waterlow's printing, Bagshawe's chain foundry and Harrison Carter's engineering works.

In 1891, J B Forder opened a lime works which was subsequently sold to the Blue Circle Cement Company in 1912. This increase in industry brought waves of people into the village and, in 1901, increased the total population of Houghton Regis to over 2,600 people.

Blue Circle Cement eventually built a cement plant near Townsend Farm around 1925. The plant became a major employer for the village, attracting people from all over the country, and continued to employ large numbers of people until its closure in 1971. Many people recall that the production of cement sent plumes of white dust over the village, so much so that the company built a second chimney to help alleviate the problem. These two chimneys dominated the skyline for many years, until they were demolished in 1978.

After the Second World War, the landscape of the village began to change. The introduction of more sophisticated farm machinery meant that fewer men were needed to work on the land, and advances in industry resulted in a proliferation of booming manufacturing businesses throughout the area.

Despite being reasonably close to London, Houghton Regis suffered little during the war years. However, other towns and cities were not so lucky, leaving over 600,000 houses totally destroyed and more than 3 million badly damaged. With service personnel returning home from the war and people re-joining their families, many getting married after being re-united, hundreds of thousands of new homes were needed.

To help alleviate this housing deficit, fourteen 'New Towns' were designed during the years 1946 – 1950, and, during the late 1950s, under the New and Expanded Towns Scheme, Tithe Farm Estate was built. In 1969, Parkside Estate was constructed, increasing the population in Houghton Regis to over 10,000 people.

Many changes were made to the original village. Houses and shops along the High Street were compulsory purchased and demolished to make way for the construction of commercial developments and a modern shopping centre, Bedford Square. In addition to public housing and industrial expansion, a great deal of other private housing was also built and, as a result, an estimated 18,000 people now reside in the town.

Today Houghton Regis is a flourishing community that continues to thrive and develop. Many charming features remain including All Saints Church, recently restored with some extraordinary help from local people. The Crown pub with its pretty bay window and thatched roof, sits proudly along the East End Road. The Baptist burial ground in which John Bunyan once preached still survives to the northwest of the town. And the Sewell Nature Reserve, Village Green and Houghton Hall Park are popular and delightful areas.

This is the story of Houghton Regis, told by the people who have lived and worked in the town during the last 60 – 70 years. I do hope that you, the reader, will find the following recollections as fascinating and interesting as I have.

An aerial view of Houghton Regis.
Houghton Hall is at the bottom left of the picture, the Village Green in the centre, c 1955 (DG)

Houghton's Hidden History

Pat Lovering

All of Houghton Regis is steeped in history. Maidenbower, for example, is Bedfordshire's most important earthworks. It is 700 feet in diameter and dates back to 3500BC. Built as a causewayed camp in the Iron Age, it was fortified by earthen ramparts which are still standing today. There were very early settlements at Puddlehill, and pottery from the ancient Catuvellaunis tribe has been found at Northfield, and there are Roman remains at Bidwell.

Houghton had plenty of good arable land and a high water table, making it attractive to Saxon settlers. It is said to take its name from the Saxon "hoe", the spur of a hill, and "tun", a village. There is a strong local tradition that the Saxons referred to the settlement as "Saelig" (meaning "fortunate") Houghton. Years ago older residents told me that this was rendered by neighbouring lads as "Silly Houghton".

The "Regis" part of Houghton's name came later. By the time of Edward the Confessor (1042 – 1066), Houghton was a royal manor, known as King's Houghton (with various spellings) or, as we know it, Houghton Regis. It was the King's demesne land, which meant that it provided various commodities directly to the royal household. It was also a rich village and paid a much higher tax in silver and kind than the King's neighbouring towns of Luton and Leighton Buzzard.

At this time, Houghton Regis covered what is now much of Dunstable, plus about half of what is now Lewsey Farm, Luton. Houghton grazing lands were the area below Blows Downs, from what is now Poynters Road to Watling Street.

At the Norman Conquest (1066), Houghton remained largely unscathed. We know this from the Doomsday Book, which recorded the value of land before and after the Conquest. Presumably King William had his royal land protected from the plundering and sacking inflicted

Memories of Houghton Regis

by his troops on neighbouring towns. Houghton appears as "Houstone, a household manor of the King's", and is included in the list of royal possessions, which starts the list in every county.

The Doomsday Book mentions a Saxon church at Houghton, almost certainly on the site of the present church. All Saints was rebuilt in the 13th/14th century, but we still have an echo of even earlier times, because for the last 900 or so years, Houghton children have been, and are to this day, baptised in a Norman font, which would have been used in the original church.

By 1100, when Henry I took the throne, the royal treasury was in a dangerously bad way, and, even more worryingly, the crown was threatened by the claims to the throne of Robert, Duke of Normandy. Henry's advisers suggested that a market town, built where the ancient Icknield Way crossed Watling Street on his estate at Houghton Regis, would be a good source of revenue. This was a busy crossroads. He could gain a steady income from cash rents for houses, shops and market stalls, and he could also levy tax on trade and the provision of food and shelter, or on travellers and traders (shades of modern times!). This idea appealed to Henry.

He kept one quadrant of the crossroads for his own use and built a royal residence there. It was completed by 1109 and was large enough for formal royal courts to be held on occasion. The new royal residence was called Kingsbury, and the King and his court visited in 1109.

Henry also saw the advantages of founding an Augustinian Priory. The clergy would all be educated men who could run the town in important ways and represent him when necessary. In 1132 the Augustinian Priory was founded, with part of it standing to this day. The new town of Dunstable was born.

Originally, Henry envisaged an area of about 450 acres of Houghton land for his market town project, but, of course, he could never have foreseen the huge growth of later years. Dunstable prospered. By the middle of the 19th century, it had long outgrown its boundaries and found itself in a position where both of its railway stations and much of its later industry were actually established in Houghton Regis.

By 1907, there was a huge upheaval. Dunstable found the constraints of its old boundaries intolerable and wanted to extend on all sides, but mainly into Houghton Regis. Houghton Regis invoked its ancient history and objected to any annexing of its land. There was a great deal of sound and fury emitted on both sides, but finally the battle was won on a question of sewage disposal! Dunstable boundaries were altered to take in large swathes of Houghton Regis, and Upper Houghton's sewage would be treated by the Dunstable Sewage Plant. The eastern boundary was also altered so that the Great Northern railway station was included in Dunstable.

Having survived the Norman Conquest and two World Wars in very good shape, it is ironic that two thirds of this thriving village was then lost in the 1960s and 1970s by Compulsory Purchase Order. The many busy shops and pretty cottages along the High Street and the 14th century Tithe Barn were swept away for no apparent reason, to be replaced by warehousing and Bedford Square Shopping Centre.

Technically, the parish boundaries were relatively unchanged until 1961, but by then huge areas of Houghton had been quietly annexed into both Dunstable and Luton: half of Lewsey into Luton and the whole of Upper Houghton (a huge area in itself); Beecroft, more of High Street North and most of Northfields, with the 'Houghton Regis' sign gradually migrating further and further down the High Street!

However, Houghton Regis has always proved itself resilient. Today it is not only quite a new shape, but it has also transformed itself into a new and growing town. It celebrates its past and looks forward to its future, and I wish it well.

Richard Hagen

My grandparents lived in Douglas Crescent in Houghton Regis and owned a nursery opening onto what was known as Dunstable Road (Houghton Road now), between Northfields School and the quarry. They were there from well before the war until the late 1950s when they moved to Biggleswade. The land the nursery was on was taken over to build a new wing at the school, so the site has disappeared completely now. They grew flowers, tomatoes and cucumbers specifically for sale in London and took them to either Covent Garden or to a big market in Birmingham every week. They sold a few locally and were involved in a bit of wheeler dealing during the war, although I don't know all the details. It was a big plot of land with about fifteen or twenty long glasshouses and a coke fired heating system that ran through all of them. However, when it became clear that we were going into the Common Market, they decided there was no point growing things in this country that needed a Mediterranean climate, because the cost of fuel was just too great and hence they sold the nursery.

I remember Douglas Crescent from when I was very small. The house backed onto the cement works and I knew quite a lot of people who worked there. There was one chap in particular, Harold, who worked on the furnaces that produced the cement powder from clay and chalk. He took me to the top of the really tall chimney when I was about twelve or thirteen years old. The chimney started off massively thick at the base and, as it tapered up, so the walls became very thin at the top. They'd finished constructing the chimney but the hoist used for building materials was still in place in the centre of it. We went up there one morning over a weekend, and it was quite terrifying. I also remember the chimney being demolished, the older one first and then the big one, quite a long time after they demolished the rest of the buildings on site.

I lived in Dunstable and my involvement in Houghton Regis was threefold really. My grandparents lived there, I used to go fossil hunting in the quarry and out with my friends (from the Manshead Archaeological Society) excavating Iron Age, Roman and Anglo Saxon sites on the Puddle Hill. This is where the quarry was dug, and by the age of fifteen I was working part time at Oakwell Park, so I had to walk down that way every day to get to work, when I wasn't at college or at school.

We found lots of things; Saxon burials in particular. The first one I remember was when I was about nine or ten. It was reported in the local paper because he was a Saxon warrior, buried with his shield and spearhead (all the woodwork had rotted away). His burial was right on the edge of the quarry on the highest point of the hill, so as you walked up the hill you had the quarry falling away at about one hundred and fifty feet in front of you. It was found when the digger cut into the side and exposed the grave from the profile of the quarry. That was very interesting – I was only watching then, I wasn't taking an active part. Over in Mill Lane and that side of the village, the remains of a Saxon village was found. It probably would have been the original Houghton Regis.

We found various 6th and 7th century buildings; what we would call huts because they were not very grand, but still reasonably sophisticated. One, which was slightly bigger than the rest, was built in a different way and was divided up very much as a church would be now, with a door at the side at one end, and then the floor on two levels running through it. We did think it was possibly a church but it was more likely to have been a hall, lived in by somebody a bit grander than the others. But one of the things that interested me most was a pre-Roman, Iron Age pit that was dug for grain storage and had been re-used to bury somebody alive. A bit gruesome - a young girl had had her hands tied up and was thrown down the hole and buried. A horse's skull was also found with her. The horse's head would have been complete when it was put in there with her, and some people would interpret this as a sign that perhaps she was thought of as being a witch, or had done something nasty to someone. Again, that was found on the edge of the quarry; so you were hanging over the edge trying to excavate it properly in a businesslike manner, in a very precarious situation.

As a group of archaeologists we always, regardless of age, found a pub to go to when we'd finished our day's or evening's work. That's where I remember going to the Five Bells several times, run by an airman whose name I think was Jack, and he didn't seem to worry whether I was fourteen, or any other age. It was a real traditional pub, situated within a row of terraced cottages. It was pulled down when they bulldozed the whole of the centre, which I think was a tragedy because it was actually quite a pretty little high street.

Mr Timms had his antique shop almost opposite All Saints Church. He was a sort of military looking gentleman, a sort of faded gentility with a large white moustache. His shop was a semi-derelict cottage with holes knocked through to various rooms and a big notice on the door saying 'Showrooms Within'. However, there was absolutely nothing that even vaguely resembled a showroom or how you expected a showroom to look - it was full of junk basically, but it was a fascinating place.

I lived in Beech Green, which was only a short walk to Houghton Regis, and went to a school in Chiltern Road, Dunstable. There were lots of interesting pubs around the area; there was the Railway Tavern at the bottom of Westfield Road and the Spread Eagle, a real hole in the wall sort of pub, with quite a reputation in the eighteenth-century. At that time Houghton Regis's boundary began at the Bull public house at the bottom of Union Street. When Waterlow's was built in the nineteenth century it was in Houghton Regis as well. They had very sophisticated but quite dated machinery and had some of the most highly skilled printers in the country working for them.

Richard Inwards was born in Houghton Regis in 1840 and died in 1937. He was at the age of twenty-one, I think, a member of The Royal Society of Astronomers, and one of the foremost experts on weather. He joined the Royal Meteorological Society and became its president in about 1895. He wrote a book called Weather Lore, a collection of

Houghton Regis quarry taken from the air, showing the extent of the quarrying around 1960 (RHA)

proverbs and sayings concerning the weather, many of which he picked up as a child living in Houghton Regis. The book was first published in 1893 and is still available.

I went to Dunstable College and was working at Rothamsted Experimental Station in Harpenden when the college rang and asked to see me. I wondered what I'd done – because you do when you're about eighteen. The vice principal told me that he'd been teaching a geology course and needed someone to take students over to the chalk pits in Houghton Regis, to explain the various levels and what the fossils were. I'd been at the College for a number of years and before I knew where I was, I was back there teaching an 'A' level archaeology course! That's the sort of thing I've been doing ever since really. I became a professional archaeologist and worked at Luton Museum and taught archaeology and history for Oxford, Cambridge and London universities for thirty years.

My archaeological and geological work was based around Houghton Regis. I also took a number of soil surveys for a group from Oxford University and the Southern Methodist University in America, gathering pieces of information on Ice Age geology, so I spent a long time in Houghton Regis.

Richard and friends starting to excavate on the edge of the quarry (RHA)

Memories of Houghton Regis

Saxon hut, Puddle Hill - This one had a bread oven built into the wall (RHA)

Most of these buildings were made of wood and don't survive - all you can find are the postholes. That's a Saxon building where we've cut the ground away – it's a hollow cut in the ground with a posthole at either end. What they would have done is to excavate the chalk, so they would have sunk the floor down, piled the chalk up all the way around and then built a sort of tent shape thatch roof from a big post at either end, with a beam across the top. There is quite a lot of evidence that they had a suspended floor, so the floor wasn't just chalk, they actually laid boards in the bottom. They weren't primitive and muddy, but were actually quite sophisticated, although the remains of them are comparatively sparse.

Houghton's Hidden History

Richard (with fork) and friends (age 16) excavating a Saxon hut (RHA)

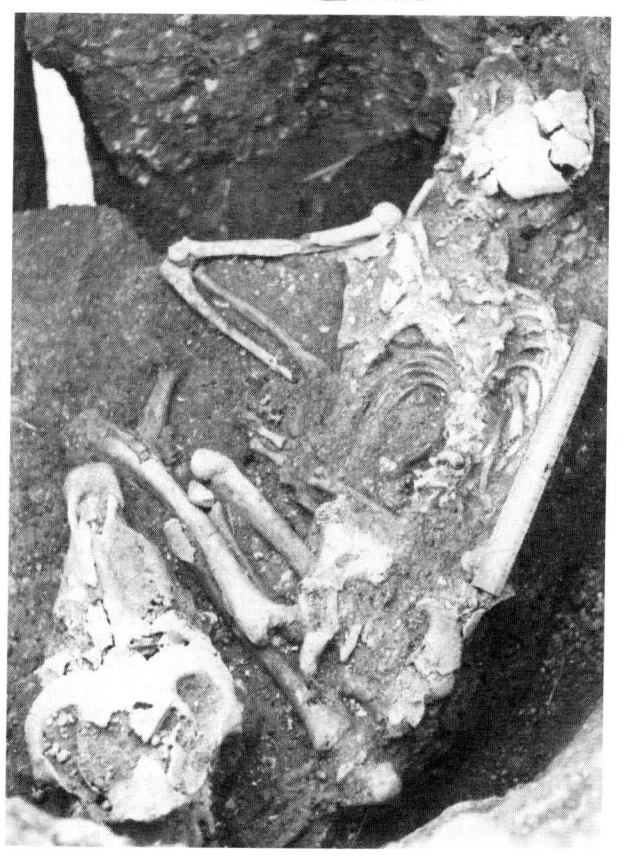

Skeleton of a young girl buried alive, with the skull of a horse's head (RHA)

Memories of Houghton Regis

Warrior with only the central part of the shield left. It is made of iron and so survived. One of the first two Saxon warriors found there. When we had finished we must have found between twenty and thirty bodies covering a 200-300 year time span and they have all been preserved. A lot of them went for anatomical examination to one of the universities, and some are in Luton Museum. (RHA)

Village Life

Whether growing up in the village, or moving into Houghton Regis as an adult, many people remember a way of life now consigned to history. With little in the way of crime or traffic, childhoods were spent playing outside in the village and surrounding countryside, inventing games and occasionally helping with the harvest during the school holidays.

Many people will remember Workhouse Row – a string of red brick terrace houses located in front of All Saints Church. The 'Lock Up' - built onto the end of the row, and used by children for a forbidden game of hide and seek - was originally used to detain the odd drunk or petty criminal, until they could be sent to Luton Police Station!

Children went to one of the two schools in the village, either the 'top' or 'bottom' school, depending on which end of the village they lived! Other activities included playing on the Village Green, watching preparations for the local hunt, collecting newts from the pond in Sundon Road (outside the Chequers pub), and playing in and around the quarry.

Originally a lime works, the quarry was purchased by Portland Cement who continued to excavate the site until 1971. Many will recall Blue Water, part of the quarry so called because of the deep blue colour of the lake. Described as a wonderful area in which to play, the intense colour was a result of particles of clay and chalk suspended in the water. Although for some, being caught swimming, or attempting to row a makeshift canoe across the flooded quarry, would have resulted in a severe reprimand if caught by their parents! Blue Water no longer exists. It has been filled with trees and shrubs planted in the 1980s to create an area that is now a combination of lakes and open fields.

Houghton Hall, a distinguished building, tucked away at the far end of the Village Green, was built in 1700 by Dame Alice Milard, daughter of Henry Brandreth, Lord of the Manor in 1654. The Brandreth family sold the Hall in 1908, when it was bought by Lt. Colonel (later Sir) Dealtry Part and his wife Edith, who continued to live there until after the Second

World War. During this time, Col. Part became Lord Lieutenant of the County and Master of the Hertfordshire Hunt. The hounds were kept in kennels on the edge of the Village Green, hence the name Dog Kennel Walk, the footpath that connects Houghton Regis to Dunstable.

During the 1940s and 1950s, Colonel Part loaned the extensive grounds surrounding the house to the village, so that the annual Houghton Regis Gymkhana and Horse Show could be staged. This event, one of the largest in the district at the time, attracted thousands of people - the proceeds of which were used to help fund the building of the Memorial Hall. Houghton Hall now belongs to a private company, who currently use the house as offices. What has been left of the grounds are now used for public recreation.

To read the following stories and memories will take you back to a time before vast supermarkets, mobile telephone masts and crowded motorways. Village retailers would send a small boy out on a bike to deliver meat and bread to customers' homes, and ice-cream was a treat that was wrapped in newspaper, rushed home and eaten before it could melt...

Mrs P Cameron

I was born in a house on the High Street in 1927. My parents died while I was a baby, so I was brought up by my grandmother.

When I was eight we moved to the Malmsey Estate where my grandmother owned a smallholding. We had three and half acres of ground complete with an orchard and six greenhouses. Five of the greenhouses were set with tomatoes – one hundred tomato plants in each greenhouse, and it was my job to water all those plants when I came home from school! My grandmother sold most of the fruit grown on the land, including apples. We had every apple you could think of; Cox's Orange Pippin, Blenheims, Beauty of Bath, but we never sold the Russets, because we all liked them ourselves and only had the one tree. We also had Williams's pears and greengages, which we made into jam.

My grandmother kept ducks and geese that she used to sell at Christmas (for £2.00 – expensive then!). She also used to buy day old chickens and kept them until they were about ten to twelve weeks old, before selling them on.

My grandfather was killed in the First World War, so my grandmother was a very independent lady. She used to have someone come in to do the housework because she'd rather be outside working. Her brother, my uncle Charlie, also lived with us. He used to grow all the vegetables, so we were quite self-sufficient. He was a very good gardener and everything had to be done in a certain way. Parsley, for example, always had to be set on Good Friday - don't ask me why!

Mum was always one for taking in waifs and strays. During the war, the Billeting Officer knew that if she had a problem fitting in evacuees, Mum would take them in. There was a big pavilion building at the side of our bungalow. The people that owned the property before us had tennis courts, and used this building as part of their club, I think. On one occasion, Mum said to the Billeting Officer, "I've run out of beds!" The reply came back, "Oh that's all right! We'll bring you some camp beds!" Some evacuees would perhaps be with us for just two or three days. One day we decided to count all the people she'd taken in – she'd had ninety two people go through the house. One girl lived with us and stayed for about a year after the war ended. She said she didn't want to go home!

We had one particular woman living with us, and one day we heard this incredible noise. Her son was a sergeant in the Tank Corps and decided to visit his mum. He brought all these tanks, about ten or twelve of them, and parked them in the road outside our bungalow! All these soldiers then sat in our garden drinking tea, with their tanks left in the road outside. I think they'd been to the Downs on manoeuvres.

At one time in the village, if you lived on one side of the church you didn't seem to have much to do with people that lived on the other side. The village on the north side of the church was called the bottom end of the village, and the school there was always known as 'bottom school' (now known as Thomas Whitehead Lower School). The school at the other end of the village was called 'top school'. They were rivals, so you only had friends that went to the same school as you!

Sometimes when we went out to play, we'd be gone all day. We'd go out at nine o'clock in the morning, and be told not to be home later than eight o'clock in the evening during the summer months. We went down to Bidwell and over to Blue Water, and played in John Bunyan's churchyard at Thorn. We used to write down all the names on the tombstones, well the ones that we could read, and we'd go down to the

Memories of Houghton Regis

Pam's daughter Christine (groom) with a friend early in the 1960s (DG)

stream near the Rugby Club to get watercress out of the wash brook. I always used to make a friend of mine lay down and I'd hold her feet while she reached for it. Then when we got home she'd get told off for being dirty and I wasn't!

Many people, including my uncle, only found out about plans to build Tithe Farm Estate when they were told that the local council would not be renewing their allotment agreements in the New Year. I heard that at the opening of Tithe Farm Estate, some of the old villagers pelted the councillors with eggs and tomatoes, because they didn't want the estate to be built. I've got friends living there now, but many villagers wouldn't speak to the Londoners for a long time.

Uncle Charlie used to work for Col. Part at Houghton Hall for a time, looking after his racehorses. I did dress-making and sewing and used to mend clothes for Col. Part, especially during the war. His butler used to send home various pieces to be mended via Uncle Charlie. Lots of things were on ration and I'd turn collars and put patches on pyjama elbows. At the Queen's coronation in 1953, I mended his dress uniform. He was Lord Lieutenant of Bedfordshire and his trousers had moth holes in them.

When my children were older I made them costumes to wear at the local village fete. They won first prize on more than one occasion...

Mr D J Dickens

I was born in Houghton Regis in 1925 in a cottage on Bidwell Hill. I then went to live with my grandparents at 22 Bedford Road. Outside our back door was a well, dug by my granddad, where we'd get our water. When my grandmother died, I went to live with my aunt at 36 Bidwell Hill - the house that I eventually bought many years later!

I went to the 'Bottom School', which consisted of just a couple of rooms and a back room. Miss Freeman was my teacher and I used to get the job of filling up all the inkwells. There was only one fire in the middle of the classrooms, so it was very cold, but I remember we were given hot Horlicks in the morning out of big urn to warm us up! The headmaster, Mr Chaperlin, lived next door to the school and Brigadier General Smythe lived next to him.

As children we used to play on the Village Green or we'd meet up in the High Street, just outside the church gates. In the summer I did lots of jobs working on the farm on Bidwell Hill. I'd lead large carthorses across the field, and helped to cut the sheaves before taking them back to the 'rick yard. Sometimes I'd harrow the fields near where the old mill used to be with a pair of horses. We always seemed to have hot summers back then. My uncle worked on Dell Farm in Bidwell, where they used to breed Aylesbury Ducks. Sometimes there were so many white ducks

Memories of Houghton Regis

Children from Thomas Whitehead School in 1932. John is in the middle row, 6th from the right (DJD)

in the fields that it looked like snow!

I used to do odd jobs for Sonny Pratt up at the slaughterhouse as a child. He used to make delicious pease pudding and faggots, and I'd deliver these for him when I was about thirteen. Occasionally, I had to deliver pheasants that had been hanging for a couple of weeks to General Smyth's housekeeper.

Sometimes we used to try and climb the ladder at the side of the large chimney at the cement works. The ladder was positioned ten feet off the ground and to try and get on it, we had to stand on each other's shoulders. We never did manage it, although we did swing on it. One morning 'Hail Mosley' had been painted on the chimney, right from the top to the bottom.

We never got into trouble and we'd wander across the fields and go wherever we wanted. We had a policeman that used to ride about on his bicycle, and if he caught anyone doing anything wrong, he'd clip their ear! There used to be a small group of us and we'd go into Dunstable on a Saturday and sing as we came down Houghton Road:

> We are the Houghton Boys!
> We never make a noise
> We know our manners, we spend our tanners
> We are respected wherever we go
> No more walking down the Houghton Road
> Doors and windows open wide
> When you hear the copper shout
> Put that stinking Woodbine out!
> You know you've met the Houghton Boys!

There have been so many changes to the village. Between the Kings Arms pub and the fish and chip shop (which used to be the Cock Inn) was an alley, called Cock Yard. My uncle owned two houses in this yard.

We had two ponds in the village. Sometimes we'd get a jam jar with a string attached and catch sticklebacks, and we'd skate on the pond in Sundon Road when it froze over. There was plenty to do in the village - we made our own entertainment. There were two chapels in the High Street, the Baptist and Methodist chapels. Sometimes when they carried out baptisms in the Baptist chapel, we'd go and watch. They used to lift the floorboards to expose a sort of pool underneath. People were then led down some steps and immersed under the water. Sometimes they held lantern lectures, where missionaries would come along and talk about the work they were doing abroad.

I was in the choir and went to church in the morning, Sunday school in the afternoon and church again in the evening! The church had an organ that had to be pumped by hand, and sometimes that job was given to me. It had a big wooden handle at the side and if you didn't work fast enough, the organist would kick his foot on the floor!

I joined the army when I was seventeen and served throughout the war. When we were due to be demobbed, we were promised that we'd all have a place to live when we came back home. But of course, after all the bomb damage there just weren't many places to live, so we (my wife and I) went to live with our relatives in London. I then exchanged that house for a place in Tithe Farm to get back to Houghton Regis, and exchanged that house for the very same house that my aunt and uncle had rented on Bidwell Hill. I later bought the house and lived there for many years before moving to Norfolk.

When I was a child I used to go gleaning with my grandmother. We went in to the fields after the farmer had cut the corn and collected all the ears of corn left on the ground – the farmer was happy for us to do this. We then used to take what we'd collected to the old windmill at the top of Mill Road, for them to grind it into flour. The mill has gone now, but part of the inner mechanism (the upright shaft) has been fitted into Stow Mill in Mundersley in Norfolk, near to where we live at the moment!

Ruth Francis-Foster (nee Baldock)

My great granddad owned properties in Queen Street, and cottages in Cumberland Street called Fern Cottage, Lyndhurst, and The Ferns. He was also publican of the White Horse pub in the High Street. After he died, ownership of his properties passed to my Gran, and not long after, all the cottages were compulsory purchased for a tiny amount of money. That caused a great deal of distress. They were really nice little cottages – very structurally sound - and people could have lived in them for a great many years. It was a big upheaval for the tenants, many of whom had lived there for a very long time. What was really upsetting was that after they'd knocked the cottages down, they then left them in heaps of rubble for what seemed like ages.

Village Life

My great aunt owned the ladies' hairdressers on the top floor of the barber's shop in the High Street. The barbers belonged to my grandma's brother-in-law, Clifford Sinfield. When Cliff retired, Sandy Reid (the business is still known as Sandy's) took the shop over and when my aunt retired, Sandy and his wife took over that part of the business too. My great granddad on the other side of my family had a hat factory in Luton. Straw plaiting was a thriving trade and many of my female ancestors did this type of work.

I went to the lower school, fondly called the 'Bottom School'. I was about eight years old when we moved out of that building and into the new school in Angel's Lane. I remember many of the little shops in the High Street including Perry's, Tansley's Fish shop and the little tuck shop where we bought our sweets. I used to go with my mum to Tompkin's the butchers, where they had sawdust spread all over the floor. There was a row of beautiful cottages in the High Street with diamond shaped glass in the windows, and a laundry on the corner of Albert Road, which always smelled of starch. It was a lovely little village.

The fair was a very big event, and I could hear the music coming from the fair, in the house in Cumberland Street where I used to live. My gran lived with her sister opposite the Green and she could sit on her settee and watch what was going on, which she loved.

I remember some of the shops in Bedford Square when it was opened. We had a Woolworth's, Bishop's supermarket, three banks, a sweet shop, post office, butchers, bakers, a chemist and the library. It was a fascination for us really when it was all shiny and new, because we hadn't seen anything quite like it before. We'd had lots of small shops in the village; the biggest of which was probably Perry's or the Wavy Line on the High Street.

The cement works was a very big employer in the area. Many of my friends' fathers worked there. It was a twenty-four hour process and I can remember being woken up in the middle of the night as a child to the sound of the midnight break hooter. It was a very scary noise for a child when all around was quiet, and it used to frighten me to death! A conveyor bucket system stretched across Houghton Road, transporting chalk dug out of the quarry, and quite often you'd find big lumps of chalk on the road!

Sometimes we'd go across the cow field and climb over what seemed

Memories of Houghton Regis

Hattie Jaques at the opening of Bedford Square Shopping Centre, 1966 (DG)

like a very large wall to get into the cement works. There we found huge ball bearings. Why they were there, I don't know, but we used to pick them up, lob them back over the wall and play with them. I can recall the big chimney being built and then being knocked down some years later. I was on honeymoon at the time in June 1978 (we didn't go away), and we watched it being blown up. The field was full of people, and it seemed as though the world and his wife were there to watch. The sound was like you'd imagine an earthquake. It was the most bizarre noise, and it didn't look like anything had happened, then, just very slowly, it started to topple, the top came off and the whole chimney just collapsed.

Village Life

The demise of the 400 ft chimney at the Cement Works in 1978 (DG/LM)

Memories of Houghton Regis

Mr & Mrs Cherry

Mrs Cherry - We saw loads of evacuees coming to the village at the start of the war. Mum came home one day and told my Dad that she wanted to take in an evacuee. A few days later she came back home, having seen a coach load of evacuees going into the school, with twin boys sitting in the front seats. She would not have liked to see her twins separated, so she went back to the school to ask if she could take in these boys. When she returned, however, the women organising the evacuees told her there was a problem. The twin boys had a sister, and their mother had instructed her not to leave her brothers – so Mum came home with three children! Shortly after our neighbours, an elderly couple, took in a young girl who my mother heard crying all night. She went and spoke to them and, discovering that they didn't know what to do with a very homesick youngster, volunteered to take her in as well!

We had evacuees all through the war. The twin boys' parents and grandparents used to visit their children at weekends. It was a break away from the noise of London. They lived near St Pancras, so you can imagine what it was like. They slept here in the house, just wherever we had room. No-one worried, for although we were at war, in many ways it was a happy time.

As children, we never slept in the house during the war. We went to an underground shelter dug by the cement company. All the children slept out there at night with an adult in attendance. It had steps down to rows of benches and bunks to lie on. Outside it was just a grassy mound, planted with flowers. Adults used to come out if it got too bad, and we used to laugh at the old ladies in their hair nets and rollers!

At school, when the air raid siren sounded, we had to go into the cloakrooms and sit on the floor. At the beginning of the week parents used to give their children sweets to take into school, and they would be placed in a tin and given out on those occasions. But more often than not, Mary and I weren't there, because our mother, who was only a little lady, came to the school and said, "I want my children and evacuees. I'm taking them home and putting them in the shelter." She didn't think it was adequate, just sitting in the school on the floor, but we didn't have any trouble with bombs. There were some that were dropped behind the hall, but not in the village.

Village Life

I can recall having to buy food and clothes with ration coupons. On one occasion, my mum bought a piglet. She brought it home and fattened it in our back garden; had it slaughtered and shared it out with family and friends. She then had the police after her, because you needed to have a licence to have a pig in those days!

My father was in the army during the First World War, but during the Second World War, even my brother who joined the army had to return home - they needed workers to make cement, especially for the new military aircraft runways. My Dad was in the Home Guard and worked his way to the top. In fact both our fathers were in the Home Guard and used to patrol together!

Jack, one of my other brothers, was in the Territorial Army. He later joined the Beds and Herts Regiment, but was captured at the fall of Singapore, and remained a prisoner until the war ended. There were also two other lads captured in the village and one sadly did not return. After the war, when we knew he was going to arrive in Liverpool, my mum was in such a state, not knowing what he would be like, that my dad travelled to Liverpool to see him.

Dad then returned home from Liverpool, on his own. Jack and his friend Ron were going to be brought back home on a train, then on a bus from Dunstable. I remember looking at this bus, and on the platform stood Ron. Well, everyone was saying, "Where's our Jack?" He eventually turned up in a taxi. We held a big party for the lads in our road. Bunting was draped across the street and the cement company floodlit our house.

The next day the taxi turned up again. The driver said if Jack hadn't been a prisoner of war he wouldn't have bothered, but he discovered a large joint of pork had been left in the boot of his car. He said he deserved this! He had obviously 'found' it somewhere along the way home!

At the beginning, we didn't know if Jack was dead or alive. He went away when his wife was expecting, and came home to see a son that had been born while he was a prisoner.

I remember the air force on the field with their radio station. They used to park their vehicles between the hayricks. We used to see troops about in the village and camped on the Village Green. When Keith was a child he sometimes used to swap a couple of eggs with the troops for a tin of bully beef and take it home to his mum.

Memories of Houghton Regis

Houghton Regis Home Guard during the Second World War. Mrs Cherry's father, Albert Maddocks, is in the centre front row with the lighter cane. Mr Cherry's father, Arthur Cherry, is seated next to Albert, on the right (DG)

Village Life

Mr Cherry – I was eight when we moved here in 1938 from Kent. On the day war broke out, I remember my father and his friend digging a shelter near the Crown Pub. As a boy I used to go up to Sundon Road track and on to Grove Farm to watch the Lysander aeroplanes. They used to fly into occupied countries and drop off and pick up agents during the war. We'd watch as they'd land, see people scurrying on and off the aircraft, and away they'd go again. It was an exciting time for us children.

We had some evacuees to stay with us for a while. We had troops from the Royal Signals who worked at the radio place in Dagnall, putting up masts, I think. Then we had two WAAFs that worked at Bletchley Park. Troops were stationed all around the Village Green in tents. On one occasion ten bombs landed in Houghton Hall Park – I think the planes were off-loading their bombs before flying on to Germany. It shook the whole house, and when Coventry was burning, we could see the glow in the sky from here. We would watch as the enemy planes used to circle around the cement works chimney before flying home.

A Wiltshire Regiment stayed in the village that did everything by the bugle; they even went for meals at the sound of the bugle in the old village hall. Some Women's Land Army girls were based near the Crown. We used to see them leaving to work on the different farms, and often saw the Italian prisoners of war walking around Dunstable.

When I started work in 1944, I remember seeing guns and vehicles parked all around the Green. On the run up to D-Day when we (my father and I) went to work in the morning the Green was full, but when we arrived home in the evening, everything had gone and the A5 was one mass of vehicles, tanks, guns and lorries, the back-up to the D-Day landings.

We worked at Waterlow's, the printers. My father had to sign the Official Secrets Act as he was given the job of printing propaganda leaflets to drop over Germany. He used to have to work on his own with a soldier standing outside with a gun. The Americans used to come to collect these leaflets wearing white helmets with revolvers at their sides, and escort them to Cheddington airfield.

I was an apprentice and helped print naval logbooks and forms. When the air raid sounded, you carried on working until the lights started to flash, before going out to the air raid shelter.

Memories of Houghton Regis

After the war I worked with a former German prisoner of war. He ran from the Russians, gave himself up to the Americans and ended up as a prisoner here. He stayed here permanently; he eventually found his wife again many, many years later after the Iron Curtain came down.

Mrs Cherry - I started working at Waterlow's when I was fourteen. I used to walk to work and Keith always used to cycle. As I walked past the cycle shed, I used to see this chap who always seemed to be pumping up a tyre, and I said, "If I was you, I'd get that mended." And that was it – that's how we met!

Michael Wiles

My Dad came up from Kent in 1939 and worked at the cement plant in the village. He'd previously worked at a cement plant in Kent and sort of transferred himself to the Houghton Regis works.

I was born in the village in March 1940. Nurse Cox delivered me - she was also in attendance when my daughter was born in 1964. I distinctly remember Nurse Cox as one of the village's main characters, riding around on her bicycle and puffing on a cigarette!

I was always told not to play in the pit. This is where the chalk had been dug from the quarry and had filled with water. But the temptation was too much for us, and we went there anyway. We used some old railway sleepers and other pieces of wood to balance on, but one day I fell in. I was soaking wet and I knew I'd get told off and didn't dare go home, so I went to the house of my friend who lived next door. Soon after, my Mum came out of our house and on finding my shoe, asked my friend where I was. When he told her I was at the pit, well, she ran straight up the road to find me. I did pluck up the courage to shout "Mum!" But she really wasn't very pleased with me at all!

Sometimes, I used to help the milkman deliver the milk. He had this little open-ended cart with bottles full of milk, but he also had a churn and people would bring their jugs out to be filled. I remember the ice cream man. He had a three-wheeled bike with a large box on the front. We'd have a wafer – a slice of ice cream sandwiched between two wafer biscuits. The man wore a white coat and a straw boater hat, and the most miserable expression on his face that I'd ever seen!

Mr Wiles, as a child, with his mother (MW)

I moved to Luton with my parents when I was eight years old. After I married we moved back to Houghton Regis in 1963, and lived in a house opposite the Village Green for about three years before moving to Dunstable. The village was quite attractive really and self-contained, with most of what you needed every day in the many interesting little shops in the High Street.

Victor & Mary Bird

Victor - I was born in a little cottage next to the fish shop in Tithe Farm Road in 1939. I remember we had to share the toilet with five other families in our row and we each had to take it in turn to clean, put paper in and white-wash the walls. I spent most of my time as a youngster playing in the surrounding fields. We'd walk over to Toddington and go scrumping for apples, play with catapults or watch the blacksmith work. Sometimes we'd go to Blue Water and catch frogs. One day we caught an injured duck, took it home and put it in the bath. When my Mother came home, she couldn't believe it! For pocket money we bred white mice and sold them for 6 pence each (old money).

Memories of Houghton Regis

There used to be a dungeon at the side of the Fire Station, where we'd often go and play. In Warren's sweet shop, if you knew them, you could get a cup of tea, cakes and lemonade in the back room.

I used to help with some gardening at Houghton Hall, and I remember that if Col. Part approached anyone working for him, they were expected to stop what they were doing, get up and say, "Good Morning, Sir." If not, they would be fired! I don't recall many problems back then. The local policemen used to give us kids a clip with his cape if we misbehaved.

In 1947 we had a huge snowfall. It drifted up to almost as high as the roof, and I recall that we tried digging a tunnel through the snow to get to school!

I left school in 1953 and started work in the local Co-op before training to be a First Hand at Clarkes in London. Working there deferred my National Service entry until I was nineteen when I was posted to Cyprus. Returning from the army, I worked for a time at the cement works. In 1963 we had another very bad winter. Many women walked to work with socks over their shoes to help them keep their balance on the snow and ice. That winter lasted from Boxing Day to the following April.

We saw many changes to the village. Lots of shops and cottages were compulsory purchased to make way for new industrial buildings. On reflection I think they made a mess of the village really. It had everything you could need and was very attractive.

Mary – I moved to Houghton Regis with my parents from St Albans in 1959. My Father managed the general store and post office in the village. He had a little van that he used to deliver goods that people had bought from the shop. On one occasion my mother was serving in the post office when Col. Part came in and demanded to use the 'phone. "I need to use the telephone!" he boomed! My mother wouldn't let him, stating that it was government property and no-one else apart from the post office staff were allowed to use it. He then shouted, "Do you know who I am?" My mother replied, "I don't care if you're the King of England. This is government property and you're not using this 'phone!"

I met Vic while working for the Skimpot Green Shield Stamp warehouse. I was sixteen and had a job in the office; I met Vic's two brothers while waiting for a bus to go to work. We met when I was

Village Life

All Saints Church in the winter of 1947 (DG/LM)

sixteen and married when I was twenty-one.

Victor – They started building the Tithe Farm Estate when I was in Cyprus. When I moved back home, I made a lot of good friends and worked with many people who moved here from London.

Mrs Beryl Morton

We came across this cottage in the village quite by chance. We'd seen a number of other cottages, but this one had a large garden which I liked in particular, especially as my father was a nurseryman in Luton. My mother came from Houghton Regis - she lived in the High Street and had eleven brothers and one sister. That was forty-nine years ago now, and the cottage is in better condition than when we moved here – at one time, I understand, pigs were kept in the kitchen!

In the High Street we had a number of shops, which really gave us everything that we needed. Of course Tithe Farm Barn was pulled down, which many of us were very unhappy about. I remember the shopping centre being built, but I don't think people's feelings about the building work were even considered. Rows of very attractive Victorian villas were destroyed, really without anyone understanding what was going to happen. I was on the parish council at the time, and my opinions were certainly not taken into account. It was Labour controlled and I was very much out of balance, being a Conservative. However, I gradually won the confidence of the ruling party and was given my full share of jobs that needed to be done, and was elected on to the board of school governors.

I helped to set up the Horticultural Society in 1960 and we organised the first spring show in 1961 – that's when I became secretary. Now I'm still the secretary, but I'm also the president! A lot of Londoners joined the Society. Many of them had left family behind and were keen to join our organisation. We had a committee of twenty-one people and it was really very good. Many committee members helped to trim hedges and worked in the gardens of a number of elderly people in the village. After the first year, we started looking after the Memorial Hall garden, now fifty years old. Our society is still very successful, holding two horticultural shows each year, a spring and a summer show.

I helped to raise money to re-build the church tower. This started as a small job, then as is often the case with old buildings, the more we went into it, the more we found had to done, till we were faced with raising £250,000. That was a big task. We started in 1987, doing all sorts of things, selling all sorts, tea towels, mugs, you name it - we just did it.

Keith & Val Wallis

Keith – I was born in Douglas Crescent in 1949, after my parents moved from Birmingham to live in Houghton Regis.

Val – My parents lived in Park Avenue after they were married in 1937. It was a relatively small village, with almost no traffic, and everyone knew everyone else. The most dangerous thing on the road was the grocer's horse and cart, because sometimes it used to take off on its own! We were surrounded by fields and farms, but if we got caught in Mr Smith's cow field, he used to chase us with his stick and we'd have to run like mad to escape!

Val - We didn't see a lot of Colonel Part, but when I was in the Guides, we used to take part in the Remembrance Day Parade. We'd assemble on the Village Green and he used to inspect us. We felt very safe, even though there were no streetlights. If you did meet anyone, it was always someone that you knew. There was no crime; you didn't lock your door. I left my bike on the Green overnight once, and the following day someone had handed it in to the Police station. I was in serious trouble and had to go and collect it with my father!

I remember many of the shops in the High Street. Perry's (that sold everything), Mr Pratt the butchers; Allan's slaughter yard; Mr Tomkins the butchers at the end of Cumberland Street, with a slaughter yard at the back. We also had amongst others, a post office, sweet shop, grocers, a fish shop and Mr Higgs the cobblers - he used to cross you over the road when you came out of his shop. My favourite was the sweet shop, probably because sweets were still rationed and were a rare treat.

Keith - I remember the freedom that we had when we were children. We didn't have to go far to get into the countryside. We were outside and active - out all day playing, as long as we were home before it got dark.

We went everywhere on our bikes and were never bored. Cowboys and Indians was a favourite game and we'd build dens on the edge of the Green - we were quite inventive. Sometimes when the hounds got loose, we'd help to round them up. The master of the hunt used to live at the top of Park Avenue and we'd regularly watch the hunt; in fact there were two, one started from the Green and the Hertfordshire hunt went from Townsend Farm.

Val - The fetes held on the Green back then were very big affairs. The bottom school did maypole dancing on May Day. I went to the other school in the village (the 'top school'), and we were so jealous of them, we'd tie ribbons round a telegraph pole in Park Avenue and dance around there! We had two events, one on May Day and the other in July, that's how the village raised enough money to build the Memorial Hall. In the very early days the fete was held in the grounds of Houghton Hall. They were quite big events; the whole village turned out and everyone would be there.

We didn't have lorries with floats at that time because people didn't generally own many vehicles then. Mr Pratt used to donate a piglet for people to win. It was then taken away and fattened up. When it was big enough to be slaughtered, whoever won got the value of it – a very big prize.

Sometimes we went to play at Blue Water at the bottom of Bidwell Hill. Of course it's all been filled in now, but a great place to play hide and seek as a child. Sometimes we used to catch tadpoles and newts and things. I never swam in it but my father did before me.

Keith – The old quarry was a fantastic place for wildlife but what I really remember about the cement works, was the huge noisy bucket conveyor that stretched across the High Street.

Val - Everything at this end of the village was absolutely white, covered with the cement dust. When they closed it, the houses in Cemetery Road doubled in value overnight!

Keith - There were some mixed feelings when the cement works closed, as it was a fairly large employer.

Village Life

Maypole dancing outside Thomas Whitehead the 'Bottom School' 1957 (DG/LM)

Memories of Houghton Regis

Houghton Regis Carnival, parading along the High Street, 1952 (DG/LM)

Village Life

'Blue Water', Houghton Regis, c 1961 (DG/LM)

Memories of Houghton Regis

King Street 1971 (DG/LM)

Val - That was the excuse the council gave for knocking half the houses down near the cement plant, that people would be better off living at the other end of the village, near Tithe Farm Estate. Of course they just took the whole of the centre of the village down. That upset local people more than anything. People were very angry to see their village being pulled apart, especially when the Tithe Barn was demolished. I don't think anyone could really believe what they were doing. There were some substantial Victorian houses along the High Street that were compulsory purchased and destroyed. Roads such as Queen Street, King Street and Albert Road were full of little houses that were just torn down.

We knew the farmer that owned Tithe Farm. He lost his home, his farm, his livelihood - everything. I don't think he ever really recovered from that. I think so much of what they tore down just wasn't necessary. They could have built the estate without touching the High Street; there was no need to destroy it all. I think people felt powerless. It didn't seem to matter what local people felt. It seemed as if everything had been decided and was going ahead anyway. But I think that was the attitude of the sixties - if it's old, demolish it. It was a long time before everyone settled down.

June Baldock (nee Sinfield)

One of my friends was the granddaughter of the owner of Tithe Farm in the High Street, so I spent a lot of my childhood playing around the farm, in the hay barns and around the cowsheds.

Renee was a very good childhood friend. Her father owned the baker's and we were allowed to go and play there. They made lovely doughnuts on Tuesdays and Thursdays! One year we entered the children's fancy dress competition at the local fete. I was dressed as a loaf of bread and Renee was the baker!

Sometimes we'd see tanks going through the village with Bren Gun Carriers and convoys of this and that. They used to park along by the Green and sometimes they'd let us climb into one of the tanks. Although it was wartime, it didn't mean a great deal to us and I had a very happy childhood.

My grandfather owned three cottages in Queen Street and two in Albert Road; after he died they were left to my mother and aunt, and were compulsory purchased – they had to sell them for a just a few hundred pounds. I remember standing in Queen Street and watched as they pulled down the house that I lived in as a child - very sad.

Mrs Dove

My husband Roy lived in Houghton Regis, first in the High Street and then in Manor Park when he was a child. He lived with his parents, Dorothy and Alfred, and his brothers and sisters, Gerald, Donald, Doreen, Gary, David and Valerie. Roy was born in Islington but the family moved to Houghton Regis during the latter part of the war.

Roy's father served in the army during the Second World War and later became a parish councillor for Houghton Regis until 1957. He was also a founder member of the local branch of the Royal British Legion. My aunt also lived in Houghton Regis. She was one of thirteen children living in a house in King Street.

After we married we bought a house at the top of Cumberland Street in 1960 for £900. We knew at the time that the house was under a compulsory purchase order, and would be bought eventually, but we also

Roy with his family (RD)

knew that it could take about ten years before this actually happened. The council finally purchased our house in 1969 for £1,100. Probably less than it was worth, but we were keen to move because my grandfather was ill and I was going to look after him.

I loved living in the village. The local shops were just a few yards away and everyone was just so friendly.

Mr & Mrs Todd

Mr Todd - I was born here in 1937 in Drury Lane, just off the Village Green. My father was chief fireman at the local fire station during the war and occasionally he would take me out on the fire engine. My parents had many lodgers billeted onto them during the Second World War – lots of different families, including a family from Malta, soldiers and WAAFs.

We had no crime in the village when I was a boy. There was one person who was a known criminal; he was a burglar and he was in and out of Bedford jail, but everyone knew him and he was the only person we knew that did anything illegal. There was a police sergeant who was a terror – very hard with us youths. He used to chase us off - he had no time for us. We used to gather on the Green in the evenings, just a group of boys, and he would come along and say, "Home!" So we'd start to move off and congregate again, but he used to come back, and when we saw him again, off we'd go, but we weren't doing anything wrong! Our biggest crime was scrumping for apples!

I used to play football for Houghton. We had four football and two cricket teams that played on the Green. We also had another pitch on a farm in Poynters Road. We kept the goalposts in the hedge because the cows were in the field during the week, and at the weekends we'd chase the cows away and put the posts up. We'd change and leave our clothes in the hedge, but there were cow pats everywhere! There was so much going on back then.

My Uncle Jasper owned Perry's shop in the High Street. I used to deliver groceries for him when I could drive. He used to open seven days a week and you could buy almost anything from him! There was no Sunday trading in those days, so he used to serve people at the back of his shop! There was a bus stop in front of the shop, and he would open

Memories of Houghton Regis

The Induction of Rev Blackburn, 1952. Perry's shop can be seen to the right of the picture (DF)

up at seven o'clock in the morning to catch people on their way to work – a very astute businessman!

Mrs Todd - You could buy anything from a needle to a haystack in there! Even on his son's wedding day he only closed for an hour!

Mr Todd – The locals liked his shop because he sold everything – he cooked all his own hams, sold hardware, paraffin and galvanised baths! He had greenhouses where he used to grow tomatoes and other things. His trading name was Perry's General Store, but the Londoners used to call his shop Selfridges, because you really could buy anything in there! He knew where everything was and nothing was priced, it was all in his head. He didn't have an electric till; he just had a little drawer.

His shop was compulsory purchased and stood empty for twenty years before they built the residential home that stands in its place now. He was furious – it was his life, his home and business. I don't know if he got a good price for the shop; people didn't talk about things like that then.

I left school at fifteen and did an apprenticeship at Hobb's Garage in the High Street. Later I went to work for Vauxhall in the engineering department. It was an interesting job, working on vehicles from the drawing board stage right through to actual development. I was there for twenty-two years, with many other people from Houghton Regis

Mrs Todd – I came down from Scotland with my mother and brother for a better life in 1961, and lived in digs opposite Pete in Drury Lane. I worked with Pete's cousin. His cousin told me that Pete fancied me and would I go out with him, and that was it really - we got married in 1964.

We had so many shops in the High Street then, including Percy Ward the baker. He created a shop out of his front room, and we'd have to queue up outside because there wasn't enough room to get into the shop itself!

Mrs Pauline Joy Baynton
My Mum, Mary Hill, was born 1924 and lived with her parents, Elsie and Fred, in Dunstable Road near the cemetery and the cement works. In

Memories of Houghton Regis

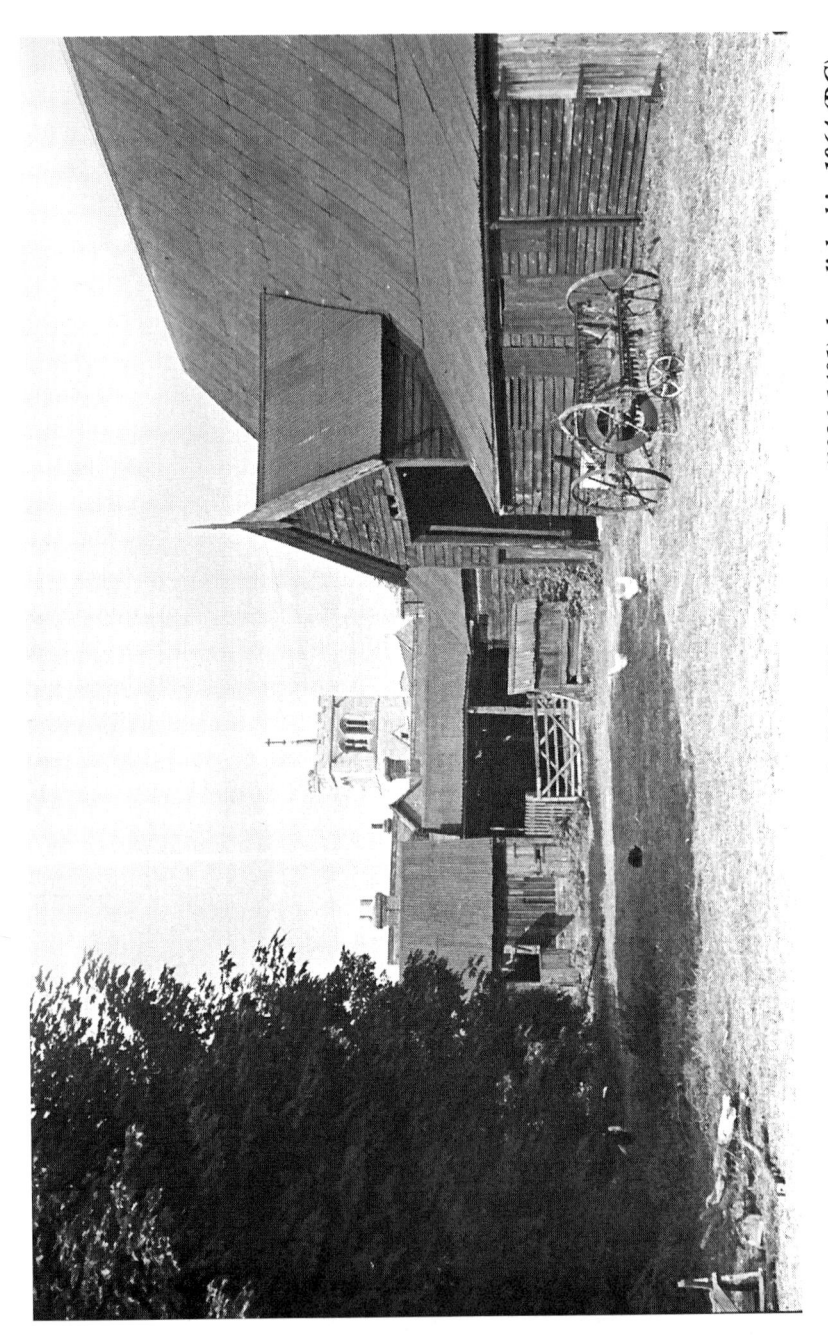

14th Century Tithe Barn, thought to have been built by Abbot John Moore (1396-1401) demolished in 1964 (DG),

those days there was no electricity, they just had an oil lamp, which stood on a table. After school every Wednesday my mother and her sisters, Jean, Joan and Norma would go to their Grandma Woods who lived near the Village Green. For tea they had mashed banana and milk with a penny Hovis loaf, followed by jam doughnuts. After tea grandma gave them a penny and they spent this in the sweet shop in Edward Street. On Saturdays she would give them all a Saturday sixpence. Grandpa Wood had a building business – he built a lot of houses in Houghton Road, and because he once worked in a bookmakers, he named some of the roads after horses.

Mr L R Dyer

There were seven children in our family living in a small cottage in the High Street, opposite the Five Bells Pub and Dickens's Shop. We used to sleep head to tail, and I was usually at the bottom of the bed!

We didn't get into any trouble but sometimes we'd climb up into the trees at the back of the Tithe Barn with our catapults, and sling pebbles at the corrugated iron roof. The farmer used to shake his fist at us and say that he knew who we were, and we knew we'd also get told off when we got home!

If you belonged to a large family like ours, it was just too expensive to pay for a holiday and if you wanted some money, you had to earn it. When I was about eleven I always went down to Grove Farm during the school holidays to help with the harvest. We didn't go on holiday; we just spent our time on the farm, helping and earning money. I was paid around 25 shillings a week then.

Terry Sharp

We got married in 1959 in All Saints Church and held our wedding reception in the Memorial Hall. About two years later we bought this house in the village. We knew all our neighbours then. Most of us were all about the same age - all in our early twenties, and we all helped each other out. If, for example, you had some bricks delivered and you started to move them, someone would come along and help you. In the end, you might have four or five couples helping you with whatever you were

Memories of Houghton Regis

The interior of 14th Century Tithe Barn (CRO)

doing.

Because none of us had any money, we couldn't afford to keep going out, so we had a kitty and held parties in each other's houses about once every two months. The party would start at around eight o'clock in the evening, and we'd see the dawn as we all went home. One of our neighbours owned a radiogram, and that radiogram used to get moved to whoever was hosting the party that night! The furniture went in the garage and, when we held parties at our house, I used to take the internal doors off, because we'd have about sixty people round. They were super parties, everyone was so friendly. A really lovely time.

Janice Enwright (nee Dunn)

I remember Col. Part - we were all petrified of him. He was very grand and to us, Houghton Hall always seemed to be cloaked in darkness. While playing on the swings on the Green, we used to talk about the ghosts we believed must have been in that great house! Eventually though, I got to work in the Hall. It's an amazing place, although I was quite disappointed when I first went inside. I expected to see a massive staircase, because it's quite a grand building. It just had a little spiral one in the corner, and then you had to go through a further set of doors to find the main staircase.

I was there for a year, working for a company called Square Meals Frozen Foods. It was the first business to lease office space in the house, but I thought it was such a shame, because the décor was lovely and they just painted all the walls and even the wood panelling in emulsion!

Pat Gidley

I joined the Tap Dancing group in Houghton Regis in 1983. I had already joined the Dunstable Operatic Society, and had to do various movements and dancing in the shows. To help us with this dancing, a friend suggested that we should join the tap dancing group in the village on a Friday evening. So we did! A couple of weeks later, she decided to leave and left me there! It was held in a building not far from Tithe Farm School, in a field, near the children's playground.

The teacher was called Hazel and some of the members were very

Memories of Houghton Regis

Houghton Hall (DS)

talented. One lady was a pattern maker who worked in London, and others in the group could sew and made beautiful costumes for us all. We put on various shows, mainly for the elderly, and held them in St Vincent's Social Club. One Christmas we all wore red and white outfits, and another time we had outfits with moons and stars all over them, but mostly we danced in leotards and skirts.

I have very fond memories of this time; everyone was so nice and friendly. It was like being part of a big family. I was very reluctant to leave, but I really enjoyed my time in the group, learning the routines – great fun!

Mr & Mrs Burnage

Steve – My grandfather was an engine driver in 1935 at the cement works, delivering cement to Luton. He originally came from Yorkshire. When his job came to a close he moved to Southampton and worked on the King George dry dock, before coming to Houghton Regis.

I was born in St Michael's Avenue and spent most of my childhood at the top end of the village playing football and cricket. We flew kites and ran about generally. I used to go to the duck pond in Sundon Road every now and then to catch newts. As lads we spent a lot of our time down at Blue Water – at a distance it looked like a lovely blue lagoon.

Iris – I moved here from London in 1961 when I was fourteen. After the war houses there were in very short supply, and countless more were badly damaged. There were six of us living in two rooms, but my father was told that if he got a job in Luton, we'd qualify for a house. There were other places to choose from at the time, but he visited Roots in Luton, got a job, and after about ten months we were allocated a house on Tithe Farm.

We lived in Recreation Road and I thought it was lovely. We had a brand new house to live in with a bathroom and a garden. In the rooms in London, we had to share a toilet with three other families, so to move from the East End of London to the countryside was paradise to me. My mother was upset that she had to leave all her family behind; her own mother was in her eighties, but I don't think she regretted moving here. However, I remember seeing a farmer being interviewed on the television who had had his farm compulsory purchased to make room for new houses to be built. I did feel sorry for him.

Mr M Sturnham

I was born in Houghton Regis in 1930 in a cottage alongside the blacksmiths, 141 High Street, near the old school. Our cottage had no running water, the toilet was at the bottom of the garden and we used to bathe in an old tin bath, which the blacksmith used to mend every now and then!

When the sash broke in our bedroom window, we'd nail coats and blankets over the window to help keep us warm. But we were happy; we had lots of open fields and woods to play in. We used to play hopscotch, whip and top and marbles. The disused cement work pit was filled with water at that time and we built rafts out of railway sleepers - we swam and took our model boats there.

I was nine when the war started, and I remember going with my mother to the Village Green and seeing the evacuees arriving by coach. My mother took in two evacuees – lads around our age; we got along really well. They stayed for about two years and became very close, almost like brothers.

There were troops billeted all around the village. The Signals Regiment stayed in the Kings Arms and the WRAFs at Houghton Hall. I saw trucks camouflaged by the vicarage, and AC Sphinx was hit by machine gun fire. It was a really foggy day when the sirens went and we were all sent home from school. I also remember seeing the Lancaster bombers flying over on their way to the 1,000 bomber raids.

POWs came in on trucks to work on the land and the home guard trained in the cement work pits; we used to watch them when I was about ten or eleven. In 1944/5 I used to help out on the farm, harvesting and helping the land army girls.

My brother joined the Home Guard at fifteen. He had a rifle at home and we ended up with ammunition all over the place! Later, my brother, together with two of his friends, joined the Navy at sixteen (their parents all signed to say that they were seventeen). He was barely seventeen when he was posted onto a destroyer in the Med in 1943. One of his friends went to the Atlantic and the other, to the Far East. All three

Village Life

Houghton Regis taken from the top of the cement works chimney c 1935 (RG)

survived. If the war had carried on, I would have joined up at sixteen as well.

I left school in 1944 and started working at AC Sphinx as a storekeeper until 1947. I then did my National Service during 1948/9. Before that I joined the Territorial Army. We were paid £9 to join the Herts Battery in Old Bedford Road. After that I worked in Luton and had various jobs until I met my wife.

We eventually bought a house on Jane's Estate. We saw this big sign saying - £50 down and all fees paid. So we borrowed £25 and with our savings, put the £50 down. I then went to the building society at Luton to apply for a mortgage, but at that time you couldn't include any bonuses, overtime or women's wages. When the company calculated our status for a mortgage, we were 2 shillings and 6 pence short, so I applied for and got a mortgage with Dunstable council.

It was a lovely village before all the building work started. Sandy's hairdresser is the only original shop in the High Street that I can think of. When Tithe Farm was built we made friends with many people from London by joining the British Legion in Houghton Regis.

Richard Woollison

My mum came from County Durham. Born in 1911, she saw a job advertised working for Col. Part in Houghton Hall. There were so few jobs around at the time that she applied for the job, got it, and worked as a scullery maid. My father came from Church Street in Dunstable. After my parents married they lived in a little cottage in Cemetery Road, nicknamed Muddy Lane. It was so muddy that when I went out for an evening, I used to have to wear wellingtons just to walk down the road. I'd then hide them in a hedge at the top of the lane and change into my shoes; coming home, I'd change back into my wellingtons again! The Co-op milkman refused to come down our road and the coalman regularly got stuck!

My two brothers and I were brought up there. We went swimming in the quarry and played in the surrounding fields. A friend persuaded me to go camping in Thorn one day. Well, it was all right until it got really dark, until the sounds of the night played on our imaginations. I told my friend that I wasn't staying there any longer, and we both cycled home as fast as we could!

Houghton Hall used to be full of snowdrops in the spring. Sometimes we'd go there with an old pram and fill it with wood. In the autumn Col. Part's wife used to collect conkers from their estate and give them out to the local children. One day my friend and I made a cart from the chassis of an old pram. We put a staple through the axle so we could turn it and took it to the top of Bidwell Hill. We both got on, and off we went down the hill. The road rushed past us and there was nothing we could do but cling on for dear life! Eventually we stopped, but we came down that hill dangerously fast. But you do these things when you're young, and there was no traffic then to get in our way! We had lots of freedom during our childhood; living in a friendly village, surrounded by beautiful countryside, I'm really glad I experienced those times.

Houghton's Tradespeople

Many varied businesses, both large and small, operated (and still do) in Houghton Regis. The village has always been relatively self-sufficient, and in the immediate post-war years an assortment of very busy shops, pubs and businesses lined the High Street. From bread to fuel, to cycles and saddles, just about everything could be purchased in the individually owned and managed shops in the village. Shop names that will sound very familiar to many residents include Percy Ward the Baker, Tansley's Fish and Chip shop, Sandy's hairdressers, Gert Smith's sweet shop on the edge of the Village Green, Pratt's butchers and Jasper Perry, who sold a plethora of goods ranging from biscuits to bath tubs!

Pubs such as The White Horse and The Five Bells have long gone, but a film still remains of the annual Beer Barrel Rolling Race. The High Street was cleared to allow the relay race, made up of teams of men from four pubs - The Crown, Red Lion, The Five Bells and The White Horse - to roll beer barrels from the Five Bells Pub in the High Street to the Village Green. With no health and safety regulations in place, spectators often had to jump out of the way of the competitors and their sometimes wayward barrels! However, it was an inventive way to raise money to help build the new Memorial Hall, still standing today opposite the Village Green. A great colour film of this event can still be seen by visiting the British Pathe website.

Richard Goosey remembers a Victorian Career Woman

My great-grandmother Mary Jane Smith was born in Houghton Regis in 1845, the illegitimate daughter of a village woman, Jane Smith, and (according to the parish register) an unknown father. It is odd that, by the time she reached adulthood, Mary Jane had come by enough capital to start a small hat-making business. The mystery of this money, and of her paternity, will no doubt never be solved.

Houghton's Tradespeople

Mary Jane and her husband, Alfred Goosey, moved into a house in Bedford Road, a little way up from the church. The family lived in the house for nearly 100 years, until 1972, when it was sold and demolished to make way for a new housing development. Behind the house, running back at right angles to the road was a row of outbuildings, principally a stable and coach-house. Over the top was a long, light room which was Mary Jane's straw hat workshop. The women who worked there (eight or ten perhaps) would come into the yard in the mornings, carrying the bundles of straw plait which they had plaited at home. Mary Jane built a brick lavatory in the yard, and for this and other reasons was considered a model employer.

In the garden, left to right: Mary Jane, two friends and my grandparents, around 1912 (RG)

Her husband, though a master baker, did no regular work but was given to drinking beer and playing cards with his friends. This happened in the coach-house on Sunday mornings while his wife was at church. One of the men would keep watch at the bottom of the yard for her return and, at this point, as if by magic, everything would be cleared away and the men would leave by the back fence.

With the proceeds from her business, Mary Jane extended the house, built an adjoining house next door, added bay windows and covered the front with fancy wrought ironwork in the taste of the time. She also

Memories of Houghton Regis

bought a number of smaller houses and became a landlady. Interestingly, a road nearby was called Plaiter's Way. Perhaps it gained its name from the local (and perhaps my great-grandmother's) industry? Perhaps it should have been called Platter's Way?

Mary Jane and her workers together with the employees of Smith & Lister in the meadow behind the house, three weeks before the outbreak of the First World War (RG)

The house next door, Ivydene (which is still standing), decorated for the 1911 coronation (RG)

Mary Jane was not a born housewife and mother. She is said to have been unable to boil an egg, and after the birth of her only child Sydney, she called for some straw to plait, abandoning the baby to the care of the ladies in the workroom, who rocked the cradle (with one foot?) as they worked their machines.

Alfred died in 1892, still not fifty, but Mary Jane lived until 1929. When I was growing up in the house twenty years later, the workroom was still full of Victorian work-benches and sewing machines, covered in dirt and cobwebs. One bench, however, was used by a local cobbler, George Robinson, and I spent hours talking to him and watching him work.

The business was too small to support Sydney when he grew up, so he worked as a manager for a Luton hat firm, Smith and Lister. He commuted to Luton by train from Dunstable North station, which he reached by horse and trap. Sydney was made redundant while still in his forties, a victim of the recession and the changing fashions in headgear. His son Bryan, my father, worked as an engineer for Portland Cement and helped to build the first cement works chimney. Later he ran his own small business.

The workroom gradually filled up with nuts and bolts, just as the meadow at the back became cluttered with unused iron girders and roof trusses. On these my mother's chickens perched, and among them a pair of geese, Solomon and Semolina, made a nest and brought up a new family every year. The trap was there too, upturned and used as a den until it finally fell to pieces.

Alan A Johns remembers The Crown

I was landlord of The Crown pub in Houghton Regis for twenty-four years, from November 1964 to November 1988.

I'm an East-Ender. I was landlord of the Cooper's Arms in Limehouse, opposite the Seaman's Mission, where we regularly had prostitutes turn up to take seamen home with them. I learned the trade from my mother. She had a pub in Wapping, The Prospect of Whitby, the oldest riverside inn in London.

We came to Houghton Regis after I took my first holiday for thirteen years. When we arrived home my wife was taken ill and ended up in

Memories of Houghton Regis

hospital in Whitechapel Road. At that time we ran a very busy pub, working from six o'clock in the morning till late at night. The doctor advised me that the long hours were just not good for my wife's health, so I rang my area manager, explained the situation and asked for a quieter pub to run elsewhere. Eventually the pub at Houghton Regis came up. At first I thought it was a seaside pub (with the name Regis) and was told in no uncertain terms by my manager to look the location up on a map!

I came to view the Crown and fell in love with it. I was only the third landlord the pub had had in a hundred years. The rent when I started was ten shillings a week, and in those days they worked what they call a 'wet rent', that meant the more trade you had, the lower your rent became. I was very happy there. Mann, Crossman & Paulin were the brewers

The Crown, undated (AJ)

before Watneys took over.

When I moved to the Crown, the staff were only paid 7 shillings and 6 pence for a session, lasting from 7.30pm – 10.30pm. Beer at that time was 1 shilling and 2 pence a pint. In London wages were much higher and so I doubled their wages straightaway - they thought this was wonderful!

There was one public bar and a very small saloon bar. The present lounge bar used to be the previous occupants' living accommodation. I put in a bay window and renovated the building. It also needed re-thatching after the fire in the 1970s. Somehow the inside casing of the chimney cracked and the fire caught the thatch from underneath. I was told that it took over twenty tons of reed to re-thatch that roof. When the builders started to decorate afterwards, they found beams with dates on them circa 1600, and I think those beams are still there.

I used to cover the public bar floor with silver sand; I used to buy it very cheaply from the cement works further up the road. Of course I had the floor scrubbed every day, but as people walked over the sand they scratched the surface of the wooden floors and that helped to keep it clean.

We had a good social life at the pub. The village cricket team was made up of people born in Houghton Regis, so I gathered together a team from the pub to challenge them. After they played they'd come into the pub for a jug of ale. One member of the cricket team, Charlie, hit the ball so hard it ended up in the duck pond opposite the Chequers pub! We formed a social club and every Christmas we used to give the old people money to buy fuel for winter. We also used to go to Jersey for the weekend to play darts and dominoes.

The Crown was a very popular pub. We would open at 12 noon on a Sunday, and at ten past twelve it would be full of people. I had no problems to speak of during the whole time I was landlord there. I only called the police twice, and that was because someone walked past and broke a window.

Houghton Regis has certainly changed. The Tithe Barn had just started to be demolished when we moved into the pub. I remember the tuck-shop on the corner of the Green, the school, where Red House Court is now and Perry's, who sold everything. There were lots of shops in the village at that time, as well as other pubs, the White Horse and the Five

Memories of Houghton Regis

Bells.

Tithe Farm was half built when we arrived and most of my customers were from London, living on the estate. I think it took about three years before I was fully accepted by the local people; they probably thought I was a cocky young Londoner! One of my biggest faux pas happened on my first day. I asked a customer if I could buy him a drink and he asked for a light and light, meaning half a light ale and half a light mild. But I didn't know this and gave him two bottles of light ale - he was not impressed!

We had a number of characters in the pub. Millie had visited the pub since she was twenty-one and was a customer of mine every evening that I was landlord. When it was time for her to go home, at around half past eight, someone would walk with her to her house in Drury Lane. On her ninetieth birthday, I asked the brewery if they would pay for us to present her with her own glass and to give her a free beer every day for the rest of her life. They agreed, and together we gave her a silver chalice and a free pale ale every evening.

The fairground people who came along to the Green were no trouble. About ninety per cent couldn't read and write, and they'd ask me to do any writing or use the telephone for them. I remember old Tom; he had a bumper car ride but would regularly fall asleep. People used to wake him up and tell him they'd been on the ride for half an hour!

The local midwife was a character. Rumour was that she powdered babies' bums with cigarette ash, as she always had a cigarette in her mouth! But no matter what time of day or night anyone needed any help, she would go and see them. She was very dedicated. Daisy used to come into the bar, and upon seeing her, many of our customers would buy her a drink; she had after all brought quite a number of them into the world.

The pub is supposed to be haunted. I hadn't been at the pub for very long when we noticed a damp patch under the carpet in the back bar. I told the brewers, they came along, dug the floor up and found a well. It had been filled in but water was somehow seeping through. They re-filled the well but we heard an old story about a young girl that died there. I had three Alsatians at that time and after we found that well, none of them would go into that bar.

I started what we called 'Wills of the Week'. Back then the News of the World newspaper would print details of various people's wills and how much money they had left, hence the name 'Wills of the Week'. Well, we all used to pay six pence every week to draw three numbers out of a bag. If the numbers you drew matched those printed in the newspaper, then you won the money. I started this game soon after I arrived and ran it until a month before I left. Some of my customers had played the game for many years, but in all the time I ran it, I didn't win once!

Renee S Hyde nee Ward remembers the Baker's

My Grandfather (Edwin Ward) was the local shepherd. He worked for a farmer in Poynters Road and my father, Percy Ward, was a baker with his own shop in Queen Street. Dad worked for an old baker in the village (Mr Sandford) when he was twelve years old, and learnt the trade there. During the First World War he delivered bread and rolls to soldiers camped on the Village Green.

When he was older, he used to play football in the Thursday league, so called because shops shut on a Thursday afternoon, giving them time to play.

My dad wasn't called up (during the Second World War) because as a baker, he was in a reserved occupation. But it was very hard work; he used to knead the dough by hand, until he eventually bought a machine to do that part of the job. He also found it very difficult to try and get men to work for him during that time. My mum worked in the shop and another man was employed to make the cakes. It was a very busy life - if we went for a picnic on a Sunday, Dad always used to take his books with him to work on.

At Christmas, if people could not fit their turkey into their own oven, they would bring it to my father to cook in the bake house. The bake house ovens were always kept alight, and he thought it would be a good idea to help some of the local people out. He didn't charge them; he just did it to look after his customers. One man arrived to take the turkey home to his wife while drunk. He dropped the turkey on the floor, scooped it up, dusted it off and said his wife would never know! I can still recall the aroma of those turkeys cooking. It was fantastic!

When I was younger I'd sometimes have friends over at night and we'd eat cakes and things in the bake house. I learnt to drive when I was

Percy Ward, aged around 13, as an apprentice to Mr Sandford c 1917 (RSH)

seventeen. I had four lessons at a cost of one guinea each and passed my test the first time. I then worked for my dad delivering bread and rolls around the villages in an old Ford van, a job I really enjoyed.

When people came to live on Tithe Farm, Dad was so busy, the ovens were just not big enough to cope. He had to make so much more bread, he didn't know where to put it – I remember it was stacked up high on my mum's table. There used to be a huge queue along Queen Street. My dad said he wished he was twenty six again with all the extra work

Houghton's Tradespeople

Percy Ward (holding the horse's head), aged 16, working for Foster's (RSH)

Memories of Houghton Regis

Percy Ward's Baker's shop in Queen Street (RSH)

the Tithe Farm residents gave him. The people from London loved my Dad's bread; it was lovely, even now people tell me that they wish my dad was still there. He made cottage and ring loaves, bloomers, long tin and square tin loaves, and won awards for the Hovis bread he baked.

Gwyneth Clarke & Beryl Lovegrove remember the Laundry and Shapria's

Gwyneth – Beryl and I worked in the Primrose Laundry in the High Street, opposite Sandy's hairdressers. Quite often on a Monday morning you would pick up a pile of towels and a mouse would jump out! It was a ramshackle old place really.

We worked in the packing department with another lady, packing laundry in brown paper with string. We worked there for quite a few years, until it closed in the 1960s. The laundry did a lot of work; much of it came from Harpenden and the villages. It had huge boilers for the washing and large rollers that sheets would be put through before being folded.

Beryl - Later we both worked for Shapria's in King Street. They made children's clothes. We were both garment inspectors. When the clothes had been sewn, we would check that they had been made correctly and at the right size. The clothes would then be pressed, packed and delivered all over the country. The cutting room was marvellous to watch, because they would cut several layers of material all at once.

It was a very good company to work for. At Christmas they would take us down to the Chequers and buy us all sandwiches. About a hundred people worked there at that time, and I think they closed the factory because they opened another factory up north somewhere.

Mr A J Reid remembers Sandy's Hairdressers

I couldn't settle in Scotland after I finished my National Service, so I applied for a job as a barber in Houghton Regis. The shop was owned by Mr Christopher Sinfield and he was such a nice man, so honest, we just gelled straight away. I came down from Scotland in 1957 and spent nine months living in a caravan at Studham, and then six weeks in a flat in Dunstable before we moved into Albert Road, which has now

Memories of Houghton Regis

disappeared, in Houghton Regis.

I worked for Mr Sinfield for about fifteen years until he decided to retire and sold me the business for a nominal sum. He kept to his word and wouldn't charge me for goodwill because he said, a lot of it was mine. I then ran the business until I retired. I still own the building and rent out the chairs to other hairdressers. My wife ran the ladies' hairdressers and now rents out the whole shop.

As a young lad I belonged to the Boys' Brigade and used to sell raffle tickets to the shops in the High Street in Fraserburgh. I'd go into the butcher's shop and was asked what I wanted to be when I grew up. Well, I'd answer a butcher, then in the hairdressers, when the question was asked again, I'd answer a hairdresser, and so on! One day the owner of the barber's shop stopped me in the street and asked me if I still wanted to be a barber. I said yes. He told me to check with my father that it would be all right to work for him. My dad agreed but told me that I would have to stay and complete my apprenticeship. And that was it; I just loved the job from the start.

When I first came here in 1957 we charged 1 shilling and 6 pence for a haircut for men, and 9 pence for boys. Mr Sinfield said that if he made £20 a week between us, he would be happy. Out of that he paid me £9 and 10 shillings a week. But of course the business just grew when people arrived to live in Tithe Farm. It was just fantastic for our business. We also had a lot of customers coming in from the cement works. Sometimes we'd have to wash their hair before we could cut it because it would be full of cement dust, and that dust would blunt your scissors quicker than anything otherwise!

We had a lot of characters visiting the shop. One customer always came in with a deerstalker hat on, one tooth only – all the rest had gone - and he used to sit in the shop with his walking stick for a couple of hours just chatting to everyone. It was very relaxed back then. I loved it here; everyone made me feel so welcome. There were just so many wonderful people in the village.

One day a customer came into the shop and asked for a hair cut. Mr Sinfield asked him how he'd like it cut. The customer just said to cut it. "Well, I've got to know how you want it cut." He said. The customer then gave the same reply. This then carried on for a few minutes before the customer said, "Well, do you want to cut my hair or not?" Mr Sinfield answered, "I don't, actually!" So he got out of the chair and came over to me and said, "Who's the boss here?" I pointed to Mr Sinfield, and off he went out of the door!

As the business got that much busier, sometimes we didn't have time to stop for a cup of tea. It was one of the things that sometimes put him in a bad mood, and it was one of the things that made him think of retiring, but I always saw the signs and kept my head down! He belonged to the Plymouth Brethren and gave ten per cent of his earnings to the church every week. He used to put little passages from the bible on the bottom of the mirrors, like 'Believe ye in the Lord Jesus Christ and thou shalt be saved'. One day, someone put a little 'h' after the 's' in saved to make shaved! Well, he threw them out of the shop – taking the Lord's name in vain! But he was a lovely fellow and generous to a fault.

Sometimes I'd open the door at half past eight in the morning and found that we'd laugh throughout the whole day, and it didn't feel like you'd done a day's work! The atmosphere in the shop was always very happy. Customers would come in and tell a joke or pull your leg, and that's what built the business up really. The Tithe Farm people came and seemed to like that atmosphere as well. It's just a case of making people feel welcome. Some customers have been visiting the shop since 1959. When Parkside and other new houses were built, this brought more customers our way. The shop itself is around two hundred and sixty years old and is now the only original shop left in the High Street.

It's been a lot of hard work, but I just love being in Houghton. It's been one long journey for me and I've loved it.

Memories of a Butcher's Boy

Peter Pratt

I can trace my family back in the Houghton Regis area for well over one hundred years. My great, great, Grandfather John Pratt was born in 1834 and appeared in the 1881 census as a farmer of 89 acres. He then appeared in the 1891 census as a farmer/butcher living at Calcutt Farm, Bidwell (the last buildings on the right after the Z bends by the Rugby Club on the way to Toddington).

He was married to his wife Emma and had two daughters, Ann, Mary Jane and a son, Frederick Freeman Pratt born in 1867, who also appeared in the above census living in the High Street. Frederick married his wife Elizabeth around the turn of the century and had three children. Two daughters, Grace, who was a spinster and lived in the village all her life, and Alice, who was married to 'Johnny' Odman who ran the newsagents/tobacconist in the High Street until the late 1950s, (next to the later Trident Maps building). He also had a son, Frederick Walter Pratt born in 1902, who was my father. My mother Edna was born in London in 1905; her father was a publican who managed various pubs including The Swan at Chalton and the Red Lion at Bidwell. My parents met when my father was delivering meat to Bidwell customers and fell off his bike near the Red Lion (by accident or design?). He was taken into the pub to have his cuts and bruises attended to by the landlord's daughter (my mother), and the rest, as they say, is history! They married in 1932 and had two children, my elder sister Pauline and myself.

Some of my reminiscences do mirror those of George Jackson in his book From Country Boy to Weatherman. Please bear in mind that I was seven years older and some of the incidents and caricatures differ slightly as we remember them.

I was born in Stanley House, Cumberland Street in Houghton Regis. Shortly afterwards we moved to Hollydene just a few doors away, a quiet

Memories of a Butcher's Boy

Mr Frederick Freeman Pratt and his wife Elizabeth with their three children, Frederick Walter, Grace and Alice, photographed in 1911 to celebrate the coronation of George V (PP)

cul-de-sac which ran down to the High Street. We had extensive gardens and orchards and the plot stretched from the junction of Queen Street right back to Cemetery Road, plus a strip of land the other side. It was a magical place to grow up in with plenty of space to let off steam and play games with other children. The High Street consisted of rows of small cottages interspersed with many small, family owned businesses and public houses. The main focus for children was, of course, the Green, where much of our leisure time was spent.

I was just five years old at the start of the Second World War and as such have very few memories of that time. My father owned a motorbike and sidecar and I can remember being taken out on trips locally. In those wartime days, petrol was severely rationed, and going out of the village to other places was a rarity. I went to the school on the Green, which was called 'bottom school' (this was on a site just to the right of Red House Court, Clarkes Way). Our school's real title was Whitehead C of E School, presided over at that time by headmaster Mr Sidney Chaperlin who lived in a house next to the school. He was assisted by Miss Laura Freeman (a distant relation to Gary Cooper!). The other school, which was situated by Mill Road, was called 'top school'.

Teaching in the school was conducted in one of two classrooms. We had a coal/coke fired standing stove and in very cold days we would all huddle around it to keep warm. There must have been some radiators but they did little to warm the old building. The primitive toilets were outside in the playground and it would be a quick dash in those cold winter months if nature called!

We were at Junior School from age five to eleven years. Education was of course basic but thorough, with discipline high on the agenda! One would not step out of line and misbehave, as a quick rap on the hands with a ruler or stick would ensue, followed by a clip round the ear or telling off when news of this got back to our parents!! However, I enjoyed my school days and luckily did not get into too much trouble!

Close to the school was Gert Smith's sweet shop and we would go there clutching our old pennies to buy Oxo cubes, sherbet dabs, gob stoppers to suck and Tizer to drink. Of course, later in the war sweet rationing was introduced, and I suspect we did not have much to chose from or be able to purchase a great deal. I imagine, however, that we were a lot healthier then, even with a restricted diet we ate well with plenty of vegetables, bread and jam as a special treat, and fresh fruit in season; such things as bananas and oranges were unheard of. Most families grew as much of their own produce as they could and shared it with others. As a family we were very fortunate that my father had a butcher's shop, enabling us, I suspect, to access a higher meat ration than regulations allowed.

My father's shop was in the High Street opposite Bedford Square, roughly where the front door of the Co-op store was before the fire of 2006. I will tell you more about those premises and associated tales of our family business later.

As a child we had simple toys and games to play. One of my favourite toys when young was a 'top'. Shaped like a bottle stopper and about six inches high with a flat circular top about three inches in diameter, with a stem about an inch across, tapered at the bottom with a smooth metal stud at the point. With a stout stick and a strong cord up to two feet in length one could, if the road or pavement was smooth enough, get the top spinning, whip it forward with your cord and send it flying forward down the street! (The gyroscopic effect of the spinning keeping it upright.) Many times we would be able to cover hundreds of yards if conditions were suitable. But beware! Sometimes with bad timing, the cord would snag on the top, sending it hurtling in the wrong direction at a good rate, often in the direction of houses and even worse – windows! However, we did not do much damage and contests were held to see who could keep their top spinning the longest. In those days the roads were our playground, as traffic was almost unheard of with the exception of buses and trade delivery vehicles.

Boys would collect cigarette cards, which would be inserted in various makers' packs, featuring the local sports or film stars of the day. Avid collectors would swap and buy until a full set was achieved. Some were very artistic and featured very interesting subjects and collections could become worth quite a lot of money, with enthusiasts having dozens of complete packs for sale or exchange. Many still exist today and now are treated as antique items. Us boys would turn up at the school playground with unwanted cards, which were made of quite stiff card, and flick them from between our fingers at the school or street wall. After so many goes, the person with the nearest cigarette card to the wall would scoop the remainder up as a winner's reward. One became very adept at judging the angle and speed of delivery and so adding many cards to our collections.

The local children would often collect in the street to play rounders with our bases at various points to form the square, but great care had to be taken not to hit the ball over fences of near-by houses. There were some houses where we knew we would not get our ball back immediately, so spare ones were vital to continue the game. To be fair, we would usually get them back in due course and I am sure that we were not too much of a nuisance. Mr Adam's house (opposite Malmsey Cottages in Cumberland Street) had a very large aviary, and as a special treat we would sometimes be allowed in to view his collection of canaries and budgerigars, and to retrieve some of our lost balls! Of course no traffic ever came our way so games went on without interruptions.

Playing conkers was always popular during the autumn season, with plenty of trees around the village green and along local lanes. Many contests were held during school term time with perhaps battles between a '34er' and say, a '22er', resulting with a winner then having a '56er'. Those battered conkers rarely survived more than a handful of encounters but it was all good fun, except when an untimely swipe resulted in a whack on the knuckles! One also had to be on the lookout for cheats who might have pickled their conker or gently hardened it in the oven... However, many happy hours would be passed playing this harmless game.

I guess that during the war years we enjoyed each other's company. We played many games of cricket and football on the Green, the focal point of the village where most children congregated. There were certain areas where we formed 'gangs' and although there was no violence, friendly rivalry existed between various parts of the village. We rarely went out of our village and a trip to Dunstable or Luton was a treat! I can remember going shopping in Dunstable with my mother; wandering around the cattle market in the Square and going to the Noah's Ark Café and ordering Welsh Rarebit (cheese on toast). Now that was a very special treat, and we may well have queued to get a table in what was a very small building. I think we had very few holidays until after the war ended, so we led a very sheltered and parochial life.

During the war we were aware that the Germans were our enemy and once a stick of bombs was released across Houghton Hall Park.

Memories of a Butcher's Boy

Considering how close we were to the Bedford Truck factory, the tank factory at Vauxhalls and other engineering works in Dunstable, we were lucky not to have been in the firing line of errant bombs more often. Boys would scour the countryside for pieces of shrapnel for souvenirs, with empty shell cases being much sought after.

We had a very stout table in our dining room and often we would be bundled under it when the air-raid sirens wailed. I recall we had an Anderson shelter dug into a part of the garden and spent time cramped on benches in a damp and dark environment; but to a child it was a great adventure! Of course the blackout was vigorously enforced, with the local Air Raid Warden patrolling the street shouting, "PUT THAT LIGHT OUT!" if anyone showed even a glimmer of light. Often there would be an encampment of troops bivouacking for a few days on the Green and along 'Muddy Lane' (which later became Cemetery Road). I expect they may have been part of the forces assembling for the D-Day landings assault. As children we just enjoyed looking at the tanks and lorries assembled before our wide-open eyes.

My teenage years started at the war's end, and I can always recall seeing my father drunk for the one and only time on VJ Day in the summer of 1945. We went to the Five Bells pub and he had obviously had much to much to drink (he rarely touched alcohol), but with the help of Nurse Cox, our cure-all, we dragged him back to the house, bundled and pushed him upstairs and put him to bed! He awoke the next day feeling very sorry for himself. I never saw him the worse for drink again...

I went on to Northfields School to complete my education, and I remember, in the years after the war, seeing lines of American trucks queuing up outside the Blue Circle cement works to collect material. At this time the 'Cold War' was still in the news and the presence of troops was very much in evidence, and of course we continued to be severely rationed. Children would scrounge chewing gum from the U.S troops in these trucks who were always friendly and generous. Getting a few sticks of gum was a great treat and really sought after, as there was little to be had from our local sweetshops. Of course, the cement works was a vital part of the village. There was an overhead cable truck system from the quarry on the opposite side of Houghton Road to the kilns and storage silos. Vast tracked excavators would extract the chalk from as much as a mile away and load it on to narrow gauge railway trucks, which

Memories of Houghton Regis

then transferred it to the overhead bucket system to the main works. I was shown around the various parts of the works (unofficially) and was greatly impressed with all the noise, heat and of course the smell of the production of lime and cement. A single track 'mineral' railway line ran from the works, connecting the Luton to Leighton Buzzard line, so bulk amounts could be transported country wide.

The other thing that also dominated the village and surrounding countryside was the 300-foot chimney, which churned out smoke, steam and cement particles over the village. Our house was right under the firing line (with the wind nearly always westerly), and my father fought the Company for many years for compensation, as the lime content would strip the paint off windows, doors and other exposed surfaces. He did get a measly sum in the end, I think, but we had to learn to live with the problem which sometimes would result in blots of material, some as big as an old penny landing on and around ours and other people's houses. In due time another larger chimney was built with better filtering equipment, which eased the problem to some extent.

We, of course, went to school either by foot, cycle or bus. The number six bus that went to Dunstable would be closely followed by us boys trying to keep up with it on bikes! A very dangerous practice, I suspect, and one that was discouraged by the local 'bobby' if he saw you. We spent a lot of our time at the Blue Water pit with our bikes. This is now a nature reserve in the Bidwell area, but in our time was a flooded disused pit and pumping station of the cement factory. Around this pit we built an up and down circuit for our bikes and spent many a long day in the summer seeing who could get the fastest time over a number of laps.... great fun!

One of the most vivid memories of my childhood was walking from the village to visit my friend David, one summer's day at Berry Corner Farm, Thorn Road, Bidwell. I was cresting the hill on the path near the afore-mentioned pit. The air was still and hot, the birds, including the skylark, could be heard singing nearby and the countryside was laid out before me in all its summer glory. It felt that I could have been the only living person on the planet at that time.

In the same area close to Berry Farm I recall, during the great freeze of 1947, skating on a solid pond of ice one evening with friends. The snowdrifts were head high with a wall of snow outside our house. Great times for us as children, and many was the time we would drag our sledges up to Dog Kennel Hill, and even further up to the West Street downs for hours of fun. We built trolleys and go-carts from wood and old pram wheels and I remember times when the Scouts organised proper races between County packs.

I also built model gliders and got quite adept at towing them up with a hand winch and letting them circle to the ground. One day I was flying my glider in the meadows alongside Dog Kennel Walk, which at that time stretched right back to the Luton Road and Blows Down (now part of Houghton Park offices and industrial units off Boscombe Road). The weather was very hot and, as it was after the harvest had been cut, there was plenty of space for flying a model plane. Unfortunately, mine got into a strong upward thermal current. I chased it right across those fields and saw it disappear over Blows Down, never to be seen again!

Those particular fields were also the scene of great excitement when the corn was cut. We would gather and watch the final section get smaller and smaller, until rabbits would dash out when there was no cover left. The farm workers were very good shots with a rifle or shotgun and would carry many rabbits away to provide extra food for the table. I can just remember, before the arrival of the combine harvester, we would help 'stook' bundles of corn cut by the tractor drawn binder. These would be left to dry out, until they were taken away to be threshed out a few days later. It always seemed that those summers were hot and sunny, and one could play outside until the fading light and hunger forced us back home. Of course, it was great when one of the local farmers bought one of the new fangled combines. We were able to get into the field to play various games much earlier, and enjoy them until the straw was set alight and the field ploughed.

During those summers we built dens in various parts of the village and attempted to make tree houses from time to time. We also played cricket, which lasted for days on end and of course during winter, football. Mates just collected as if by magic and many improvised games were invented with us all letting off steam and tiring ourselves out. One of our favourite things to do was to ride our bikes along 'Rabbit Lane' (skirting Houghton Hall grounds), then go into the edge of the Hall grounds through the trees and finish at the bottom of Poynters Road where Portz Avenue now finishes. We had to keep a lookout for the Hall gamekeeper who, if he was about, would shout at us to "Clear off!!" To my knowledge there was no vandalism or anti social behaviour, and bikes and playthings could be left around without fear of theft. Happy days!

I joined the Cubs and Scouts, I went to All Saints Church and sang in the choir and, later in my teens, learnt to ring the bells. One never seemed bored…there was no television, but we would rush home when Dick Barton, Special Agent was on the radio. We were enthralled by him, Snowie and Jock and their exploits, and re-lived their adventures in play. A special treat was to go to the Union Cinema (now Cubes) in Dunstable on a Saturday morning and be one of the ABC minors, watching films such as Tarzan and Laurel & Hardy and, sometimes, live entertainment. The manager/owner was a friend and customer of my father, so as children we would often receive free tickets (no doubt exchanged for extra rations of meat, I suspect!).

Most boys collected train numbers, and we'd set off with our Ian Allan book, which listed by engine class, all the steam locos of the day. Many Sunday afternoons would be spent on the railway bridge on Sundon Road with a tennis ball, playing football in the road. If one was not careful a miss-kick would result in the ball landing in the cutting below, and a long retrieve would ensue. If a dozen cars came by during our three-hour stay, it was considered busy! We'd get a packed lunch and cycle to Leighton Buzzard and spend the whole day there, marvelling at the speeding trains belching steam and soot just a few feet away from us. When British Rail came into existence together with the advent of diesel engines, most of the glamour went out of our hobby and we spent less time at this pastime. However, I still have my original dog-eared collector's book. Many boys went fishing (which never appealed to me), and would cycle to the local canals to pursue their hobby.

I was always interested in sport and enjoyed keeping fit by running around the countless footpaths and lanes that abounded nearby. I was very much into cricket and would spend countless hours by the small pavilion that served both as a changing room and scorer's hut. If one was lucky the visitors would not have brought a scorer along, and it enabled me to test my maths out, having to balance the score book with our own team's scorer. We had a very strong team in the village and were one of the best in the area, with some very big hitters and good fast bowlers. I can remember one in particular, Dicky Bird, who had the most unusual run up, but as a medium pacer was so accurate that few runs were ever scored off him, and his nagging length and ball movement bought him countless wickets. Likewise Ray Birchley, who with Dicky proved many a downfall of opposing sides. Sometimes we would help the groundsmen push and pull the roller used for wicket preparation and when extra weight was needed, we would be allowed to ride on the roller's box frame!

I eventually graduated into the side and many happy days were spent playing my favourite game into my forties, usually opening the batting and loving every aspect of the game, particularly the Ludun Cup, a twenty overs knockout competition against all the local sides.

We also had a very good football team and many Saturday afternoons were spent watching them on the Green. I also played for the village football team as a rather mediocre right-sided forward...but always enjoyed it! In those days the teams changed in the British Legion Hall on the Green (behind the site of the present Memorial Hall). It was spartan to say the least, but we made do. For many years this site was the home of our Youth Club, where we could enjoy table tennis and other games, and where whist drives, dances and other social activities took place.

I remember when the present Memorial Hall was planned, we had to remove a large tree stump at the front boundary. With only hand tools and sweated labour we seemed to spend weeks getting it out in our spare time and succeeded in the end, to much celebration! I was lucky enough to serve on that committee for many years with other stalwarts like Russell Somerton and his wife Doris, Jim Caldwell (Secretary), and numerous other dedicated members. I can recall in later years after Russell died, Doris, who lived at the last house in Bidwell (by the now Rugby Club), used to walk all the way up to the Memorial Hall on Wednesday and Friday bingo nights, carrying the necessities for refreshments and raffle prizes well into her eighties - true civic duty!

From my early teenage years I was a competent card player and enjoyed playing at local whist drives. I'd catch the bus to play at Tebworth village hall and Tilsworth church hall on Saturdays. In my later years I ran a Monday whist drive at the Memorial Hall for over thirty years and helped out calling on bingo evenings. In the village there was a small room in Albert Road (which ran from the High Street opposite Sandy's hairdressers to Queen Street). This belonged to the Women's

Memories of Houghton Regis

British Legion who organised whist drives and other social events, but if you got more than twenty people into that room you were very lucky!

Other people stick in my mind as being part of the fabric of the village; Wally Upton was the local road sweeper, a gently quiet man who went about his work slowly but efficiently. Lol Bright, caretaker/boiler man at the church and the old British Legion Hall. Arthur Inwards (known as the midnight milkman on account of his very late deliveries during the day/evening). Mr Townsend, the butler at Houghton Hall and Fred Hawkes, the coalman and ice cream man who was always dressed in a long white coat and straw boater. He appeared with his tricycle in the summer, having come from Fossy's ice cream works in Leagrave (opposite the Archway Bridge). We would rush home to get money to buy a delicious wafer treat. Roses Dairy from Wingfield were well known in the village, once it had expanded to take in the Tithe Farm Estate in the late 1950s.

I also remember the Reeves family at the Chequers, Ted Ledo at the Crown and the Thorpe family at the Five Bells, whose daughter Betty was a talented lady and local journalist, and was a part of the local life and times. Someone who appeared from time to time was a local tramp called Coal Black Charlie, who would scare the pants off us when he appeared walking down the High Street from Dunstable. He might knock at a few doors – he had one or two people who he knew would give him some scraps of food. We would never approach him, but sometimes taunt him from a distance with words and cat-calls, and he would respond by making towards us and send us running.

One of the sights of the village in the late 50s was the parade of the local hunt hounds, kennelled by the Green. They were exercised with the huntsman in his scarlet coat astride his horse through the village, with a white-coated 'whipper-in' walking behind to ensure that all the hounds were kept in check. Understandably there was so little traffic about that disruption to village life was minimal and folk would gather and watch as this parade passed by. No chance of that now!

Similarly, I recall in the 50s and 60s, when we had the Village Fete on the Green, a beer barrel-rolling race was held. The course varied from time to time, but I remember the ones that ran from the Five Bells pub (near where Netto is now), down to the Green, with the finish on the road leading to Houghton Hall. The race was a relay with teams of four stalwart regulars from four pubs. One year we were approached by the

Memories of a Butcher's Boy

The North Hertfordshire Hunt by the Village Green.
The chimney of the cement works can be seen in the background (left) (DG)

Memories of Houghton Regis

Beer Barrel rolling race held at the Village Fete 1957 (DG/LM)

Memories of a Butcher's Boy

Pathe newsreel company to film the occasion, and I was given the task of driving the camera-man in the back of Dad's Bedford Dormobile van. We secured the doors wide open and preceded the race at a pace just in front of the leading competitor. The resulting film was later shown at the Union Cinema, much to the joy of the Fete committee.

Traffic was held up at Bedford Road and East End until the race had passed, and anyone watching on the pavement had to be very careful, as sometimes the barrels would take off at angles and career towards the crowds nearby! I don't think Heath and Safety issues would ever allow it now, but at the time it was all in good fun and any small cuts and bruises usually sustained by the 'pushers' were soon dealt with...all good entertainment. The Fete itself was always well supported and was generally organised by the Memorial Hall Committee. As a younger boy I can just recall a much larger event with show jumping and a quite grand event in the grounds of Houghton Hall.

I will now recount some of my memories connected with our family business:
As I have indicated earlier, butchering in our family goes back to the late 1800s. My grandfather, Frederick Freeman Pratt established the shop in the High Street, opposite Bedford Square. There were three cottages stretching back from the frontage. The first cottage became the shop; the second became living quarters for my grandparents (and later for my Aunt Grace and 'Aunt' Eva, a distant relative), the third cottage was mostly unoccupied and was used as storerooms. At the rear was a bake house, which I assume was used by the business in some form or another until it was converted to hold a walk-in refrigerator. There were three staircases and interconnecting rooms, so it was possible to get from the front to the rear of the premises either at ground level, or on the first floor without going outside. Very useful as children, if we were playing hide and seek!

At the rear of these buildings were a number of barns with lofts to store straw, etc. When these were filled with straw bales, games could be played and dens built, much to the delight of mates invited round to play. There was also a small slaughter house where we would kill and dress our own animals. A large vegetable garden led down to pigsties and larger barns, which housed ducks and chickens. Beyond this was a large

Memories of a Butcher's Boy

Our Butcher's shop in the High Street (PP)

field with barns used as chicken houses. In total it stretched from what is now the end of Whitehouse Close and over towards Clarkes Way. As children, it was a magical place to roam around, and we had adventures and played games to our hearts' content.

I remember collecting eggs from the many egg laying compartments, which could be accessed from outside by lifting a hinged hatch. Father was a skilled rearer of poultry and pigs and it was a great pleasure watching a large sow feeding many piglets. Great care was taken to ensure that the mother did not crush any of her brood when laying down to feed them or getting back up, and a safety bar was erected so that the little ones could scamper out of the way and be somewhat protected.

We had a very large metal boiler built into a brick surround, heated from below by an open coal fire. In this pig's swill would be cooked, consisting of unused food scraps, both meat and vegetables, bought in supplements and other bits and pieces resulting from the slaughtering process. The resulting smell was often quite obnoxious, but the animals seemed to thrive on it and never came to any harm as a result. In those days even the gut of slaughtered pigs would be cleaned out to make sausage skins, and I recall my Aunt Eva with a bucket and hose cleaning and scraping to ensure a safe product. The large intestine and stomach would be similarly treated and cooked and turned into chitterlings. My father had a saying that the only thing you didn't use from a pig "was its squeal." In those days especially after the war, nothing was wasted, and many of the resulting products were sold 'off ration' to the benefit of all.

He would buy the cattle needed for slaughter from the local markets at Dunstable, Leighton Buzzard, Luton or from farmers who would let him know when beasts were ready and suitable. My father was rarely called Frederick or Walter, his given names, and then only usually by more elderly lady customers. He was known by all as Sonny Pratt, (I expect that was a corruption of 'son of' to distinguish him from his father.) He told us that as a young boy he would have to go to Leighton Buzzard on his bike and drive a bullock all the way back to the shop after it had been bought by his father. He also recounted the time, usually Sunday evening, when cattle from the Bunkers' farms north of the town would be driven en-mass down Watling Street through the chalk cutting to the railhead at Dunstable North station, then onwards to more distant markets. Often we received a delivery of live animals, bought by Dad at the local market via cattle trucks. It was quite a squeeze to get a large lorry up past the buildings and into position for unloading... We then had to ensure that the way down to the meadow was blocked off and the door to the barn where they would be kept until slaughtering was open. As soon as the rear doors of the lorry were opened the animals would emerge! Of course some would be very docile, and with a few reassuring prods, would proceed quietly to the barn. However, there were often times when the cattle were quite stressed and very lively. On many occasions this would result in much shouting, waving of sticks or boards to encourage them to go in the right direction. Often the load of animals would have been bought by other butchers and needed to be sorted, and sometimes a rushing beast would brush our efforts aside, burst through our defences and make off down the field. Even worse, a particularly nasty bullock would sometimes back track and get by the rear of the lorry and escape towards the High Street! Calamity ensued, and the beast would be pursued by us all. I'm pleased to say that we always got the animal back safely and usually without harm to people or property, but it was quite hairy at times. Nevertheless, the animals were always well treated and kept in good condition before being slaughtered, as this was essential to ensure the quality of the finished product.

The use of butchers' slaughterhouses was eventually stopped by government regulations in the 1950s, and it was the one thing that I never learnt as part of the trade. I must say that the conditions seemed rather primitive compared with modern techniques and standards, but most butchers produced a first class carcase, and great care was taken to ensure the best quality of finish so that the final product on his counter was as good as it could be. After all, his reputation was on the line!

I would help as a boy delivering customers' meat orders on a Saturday. Together with my cousin Barry Meachem we had about three rounds to do; mine was towards the Dunstable end of the village, and his towards the Green and East End. Our carrier bikes were fitted with wicker baskets and we would pack the orders in reverse order and separate each layer with greaseproof paper. We then loaded our heavy baskets onto the carriers, ensuring that pressure was always kept on the rear of the bike so that it didn't tip up! We then proceeded on our designated rounds, taking great care not to hit any kerbs or obstructions, and when at the appointed house, make sure that the bike and load was very secure. We had a small wicker basket to carry the order to the house and collect the necessary money. There were a couple of times when slight accidents occurred but I'm glad to say we both had a very good record. A tip was often given and at the end of the day we would cash up our takings with my mother and balance the books. In today's climate of environmental health and safety, I'm sure that our way of delivering meat would not be allowed, but as far as I can recollect we didn't poison anyone!

In those days customers were very cost conscious and our prices had to be kept in line with what was being charged elsewhere. Most families would buy a roast for the weekend and make it last for two days (we were never open on Mondays). They would usually shop every day of the week for each day's dinner, as household fridges were unknown then, and you could set your clock by the time some customers would appear daily. I can remember when the ration was ten old pence per head and you were assigned to register with a certain shop. When a few items arrived that were 'off ration', the shop would rapidly fill with customers queuing to purchase those few extra goodies. During the rationing period and after the small slaughterhouses were closed down, most of the local meat was obtained from the Griffith's Brothers slaughterhouse in Victoria Street, Dunstable. This was under the guidance and control of local officials who allocated meat to each business, according to how many customers they had registered with them. I suspect there may have been some persuasion to obtain more than one's allocation, in return for some favours!

Father fell foul of the law once - as a result of killing one of his own pigs illegally during the rationing period, (when all produce should have been pooled and shared out). The carcase was cut up and hidden in the cellar, but I suppose someone may have overheard conversations between father and potential customers of the pork because, as a result, he was visited by the law, the meat was discovered, and he was fined as a result. I suspect that this type of thing may well have happened in many other businesses but was never discovered...however, I think he learnt his lesson.

****

I completed my National Service in 1954, at around the same time as the Tithe Farm estate had finished being built. I told my father that, although I didn't want to break away from the business, I'd like to run a business of my own. So I bought a mobile shop to service the houses on Tithe Farm, as there were no other shops built on the estate at that stage. I bought my own meat separately and stored it in my father's premises, but ran it as a separate business. I did that until shops were built in Harborough Crescent. I then took a lease on a shop and continued to run a couple of mobile shops for about ten years. After my father retired I took over the running of his shop. A few years later his shop was compulsory purchased and knocked down to make way for what is now the Co-op site.

There were two or three other mobile shops that delivered goods to the estate, because at that time a lot of the village shops had already

Peter Pratt's Butcher's Shop and Mobile Shop in Harborough Crescent (PP)

been compulsory purchased and had gone. When the buildings in the High Street were knocked down, people generally thought that it was fait accompli really. The local council said that industry needed to be developed and things had to change. In those days there were no pressure groups to try and challenge those views and at that time, after the war, people were anxious to see things improve. Of course, today those buildings would be preserved. But rows and rows of old cottages and picturesque areas were taken down and levelled, and people basically just stood by and watched. We didn't seem to have any clout in saying what should be happening. But it was a time of great change after the war; things were traumatic and people wanted to see things emerge that perhaps would be better.

We got on very well with the people on the Tithe Farm estate. They were different, jolly and generally young people with families. We had a lot of good vibes, they were very friendly and we had a laugh and a joke with them. I don't think there was initially a great deal of interaction between the old and the new people in Houghton Regis, and to some extent it changed the nature of the village, because obviously it was going to get much bigger. I felt they were well accepted, they joined in with village life, as there was very little else to do. They moved in gradually as the houses were built and the roads were completed, and it was quite interesting to see. I think it was quite a culture shock for many people, though. There were no shops or amenities on their doorstep and it must have been strange being in a backwater such as Houghton Regis.

I decided to sell my business when I was in my early fifties. I sold the lease to another butcher and came into Dunstable and started a wholesale business for another ten to twelve years. I then leased another small shop in Dunstable until I retired.

Our family were always acknowledged as tradesmen in the area, and our family name is well still recognised by many of the older generation in the village.

Above: Entrance to Houghton Hall Park   Below: Houghton Hall (SK)

Views within Houghton Hall Park (SK)

Above: Picnic area, Houghton Hall Park   Below: The Kitchen Garden (SK)

Memorial on the Village Green (SK)

All Saints Church (SK)

Houghton Regis Old Cemetery (PL)

Above: View to Crossways (PL)   *Below:* The Chequers Pub (SK)

Above: The Memorial Hall   Below: The Village Green (SK)

Journey to the Other Side of the World...

If you have ever thought about tracing your family history, take a look at the following story of one family from Houghton Regis who travelled to the other side of the world...

Geoffrey Tompkins – My Ancestors: Citizens and Tradespeople of Houghton Regis

William Tompkins was born in Houghton Regis in 1802. He became a shoemaker and married Mary Humphries. They had several children, one of whom was Joseph, born in 1827. On December 26th 1847, Joseph married Sarah Cook at All Saints Church, Houghton Regis. Another brother was George Tompkins who was Clerk to Houghton Regis Council for sixty-four years. This is mentioned on his gravestone situated on the east side of Houghton Regis churchyard.

There was also a sister, Jane Tompkins who became a bonnet sewer. On 23rd August 1860, at All Saints Church, she married Jeremiah Barrett, a miller from Great Chesterfield, Essex. They then travelled to Muswellbrook, on the east coast of New South Wales known as "The Gold Coast", one hundred or so miles north of Sydney, Australia. In 1862, a son Walter was born, he became a carpenter and another brother William, a wheelwright in St Peter's in Sydney.

By the 1881 census Jeremiah, Jane and a daughter Annie aged twelve years were back in Houghton Regis at Whitehorse Street. Sometime after this Jane dies, and on 18th June 1888, Jeremiah married a young woman called Elizabeth Fletcher, again at All Saints Church. The first marriage certificate indicates Jeremiah to be thirty-three in 1860, the second, fifty seven in 1888, so maybe he was either getting younger or perhaps he was not sure how old he was, as he was born before the requirement for birth certificates! More likely he did not want his young bride to know how old he really was!

Memories of Houghton Regis

Joseph and Sarah Tompkins moved to Dunstable sometime in the 1850s. Joseph Tompkins was a hat blocker and Sarah a bonnet sewer. The daughters also became bonnet sewers. The eldest son William appears to have emigrated to Melbourne in Australia and settled in the Brunswick area. In 1862, another son George Tompkins was born. He became a carpenter and in 1882 married Elizabeth Cooper of Tilsworth, Bedfordshire – daughter of Abel Cooper, a Tilsworth farmer. Elizabeth Cooper was first cousin of Charles Cooper (father of the American actor Gary Cooper).

George and Elizabeth had a son William Murray Tompkins born in 1882. Murray was probably named after the Murray River, which separates Victoria and New South Wales, where relatives and friends were probably writing back from.

Walter Barrett and George Tompkins were both carpenters and also first cousins. Walter Barrett appears on the sailing register of the Lusitania (an earlier ship to that torpedoed by the Germans in 1915), arriving in Australia in April 1883. George Tompkins left on a sister ship, The Chimborazo, arriving in Melbourne on 3rd June 1883. He wrote a comprehensive diary of the voyage.

In 1885 Annie Elizabeth Tompkins (George Tompkins' wife), Annie Tompkins (sister of George Tompkins), Arthur E Tompkins (brother of George) and William Murray, son of Annie Elizabeth and George, arrived in Australia on the Lusitania.

George Tompkins and Walter Barrett went into business as house builders and carpenters in New South Wales. For a time they lived next door to each other in houses which they had built in the late 1880s at Holden Street South, Sydney, New South Wales. By about 1890 Walter Barrett was back in Muswellbrook, operating as a building contractor, where he prospered and became very successful into the mid 1920s when his company became Walter Barrett & Son, and then he probably retired. He purchased substantial land and holdings, creating and granting mortgages on disposals. These are listed in the Torrance Land Register in the Sydney archives.

Meanwhile Annie Elizabeth Tompkins, wife of George, had given birth to two further children, Lily and Ivy, and in 1892 went home for a holiday to England with her children. She died of enteric fever at Watford, Christmas 1900 and is buried in Tilsworth churchyard. The other Annie Tompkins (sister of George) also went back to England (it may have been at the same time), and died a spinster in Dunstable in the mid 1920s.

Meanwhile George Tompkins, who lived at Holden Street South, (Walter Barrett's house having been let whilst he was in Muswellbrook) contracted TB. He died on 13th July 1894 of TB, pneumonia, and exhaustion at the Royal Prince Alfred Hospital in Sydney. He is buried at St Peter's churchyard in Sydney. It is thought the other brother Arthur E. Tompkins probably returned to Dunstable at some time.

By 1929 Walter Barrett was sixty-seven and probably retired. He donated a sum of money to have the turret clock in the Tower of All Saints Church, Houghton Regis, replaced. He also paid for a brass plaque to be placed on the southern wall of the Tower, indicating that he donated the clock in memory of his father Jeremiah, who was associated with the old clock for twenty years. The plaque is still there today. Walter Barrett obviously remembered Houghton Regis, the home of his mother's family for many generations, and thus donated the clock.

Brass plaque on the wall of the Tower of All Saints Church, donated by Walter Barrett (GT)

Memories of Houghton Regis

The following transcript is that of the diary written by George Tompkins in 1883 of the voyage of the Chimborazo, initially to Melbourne. The Chimborazo then carried on to Sydney where the passenger manifest is retained by the public records office at The Rock, where it can be seen that George Tompkins signed himself off the ship.

VOYAGE OF THE SS CHIMBORAZO FROM GRAVESEND, ENGLAND TO SYDNEY N.S.W. AUSTRALIA, WRITTEN BY GEORGE TOMPKINS

Thursday 19th April 1883

Voyage of the SS Chimborazo from Gravesend, England to Sydney NSW.

The vessel started on Thursday 19th April 1883, but previous to going on board I determined to keep a few notes on the way, partly to pass away some of my leisure hours, and partly because I thought it would interest some of the friends I left at home, if I gave them a full account of my experiences should I arrive safely.

I arrived at Gravesend at eleven o'clock on the 19th April, having travelled from London by train. As soon as I could get my luggage, I hurried down to the wharf where I found a steam tender already waiting to take passengers to the Chimborazo, which was laying at anchor in the middle of the river between Gravesend and Tilbury.

In a very few minutes we were all on board. I, having disposed of my property and taken possession of my bunk, by placing my blankets on the end that bore the same number as my ticket, hastened on deck to take a look around, and to have a final chat with those who came to see me off. In about half an hour the bell rang, as a signal for all visitors to quit, so I was very soon left a stranger amongst strangers. I then took a ramble round the ship from stem to stern, and by the time I had completed my inspection the dinner bell rang, and I for one was very pleased to hear it, as the sea air being new to me, gave me a rather keen appetite. But also the sea or the effects of it, very soon affected me in a manner less pleasant. But of that further on. I found plenty of amusement all day by watching other vessels passing us down the river. But we did not actually start on that day, as we had expected to do, so I retired very early to sleep for the first time with water all around me.

Friday 20th April 1883

I arose this morning at five o'clock not very much better for my night's rest. The situation was so different to anything I had before experienced that I could sleep but little. However, I felt somewhat refreshed after a good wash. I went on deck, but to my sorrow I found it raining fast. We had a very early breakfast, after which I again went on deck to have a last look at Gravesend, rain or no rain. But what was my surprise to find that Gravesend was already a mile or so behind. The anchor had been drawn up and the ship set in motion, under easy steam, but so intent was I upon satisfying the inner man that I had not noticed it, nor had any of the others at the same table.

Now we continually passed barges, large and small sailing vessels and boats of all kinds, and as we had land on both sides of us, we were not at a loss for something to look at. As we steamed along we could see several forts built upon riverbanks, and a gun fired as we passed each one of them, but why, I did not find out. By 12 o'clock we lost the land on the north side, or rather the port side. But we kept in sight on the starboard, passing in quick succession Margate, Broadstairs, Ramsgate, Deal and Dover. At Dover the view was very pretty. The cliffs rose from the sea, high and white, and on the top but some distance back, stood a castle. As we passed four flags were run up the mast head to let them know who and what we were.

Beside the castle there were other forts at Dover, and we could see many large guns pointed towards us. But we soon left it all behind, and our speed increased as we had more room. By this time too the weather was much finer, but a very strong wind was blowing, and by 7 o'clock I began to feel anything but comfortable, and I considered it would be wise on my part to go to bed, and this I very soon did. I slept well.

Saturday 21st April 1883

This morning the view from the deck was very interesting. We were very close to the Devonshire coast. At 10:30 we entered Plymouth sound and as soon as we had passed through the breakwater (at the end of which stands the lighthouse), the anchor was let down, and we were once more in quiet water. In about half an hour a small steamer came alongside, bringing us more passengers. A missionary came on board with them, not with any intention of going abroad, but just to have a short service after distributing a few of Sankey's hymn books. We all sang that very beautiful hymn 'I love to think of that heavenly land where parting is no more'. Then the preacher prayed for the friends who would soon be left behind, and for us that were going away, and lastly that the captain, and all those who had management of the ships, might have wisdom and knowledge to take her safely, to that other land to which we were all bound. We then sang another hymn or two, after which the missionary spoke to us in a few well chosen and appropriate words. He then retired in the small steamer, having cheered us wonderfully.

In another hour or so we lost sight of dear old England, our birthplace and the home of our nearest and dearest. Towards evening the wind blew very hard, and the motion of the boat became unpleasant, and about seven hours after leaving Plymouth, I had to pay the penalty, inflicted upon nearly all landsman taking their first voyage, or in other words, I became very sea sick, and was only too glad to turn in.

Sunday 22nd April 1883

To my surprise I slept well, but to say I felt queer when I got up would scarcely express my feelings. I felt giddy, sick, everything except hungry. I did not rise until breakfast was over, and as we were now in the Bay of Biscay, and nothing but water to look at, I went to bed until dinnertime, and then again to teatime. I then went on deck for a couple of hours, and tried hard to persuade myself that I was much better. But as the wind had increased, and the waves were washing over the portholes, this was a failure. The sailors considered this very smooth for the Bay of Biscay. As I lay in bed that night listening to the wind and waves, my thoughts wandered back over the way we had travelled, and my friends were constantly in my mind as, I suppose, I was in theirs. But even these thoughts, pleasant as they were, could not keep me awake.

Monday 23rd April 1883

We were now out of the Bay, and were sailing off the Portuguese coast, but so far off, that we could only occasionally catch a glimpse of the distant hills, and they were so indistinct we could scarcely distinguish them from the clouds. The weather was very fine, and we had a good stiff breeze, blowing from the right direction so that we made 310 miles in twenty-four hours. All our sails were set, and we went along in fine style. About 9pm we sighted a revolving lighthouse. It was situated near Lisbon, or somewhere between Lisbon and Cape St Vincent, but I am not certain of the exact spot.

Tuesday 24th April 1883

The weather was still very fine, and upon looking into the sea, I found that we were being piloted by a shoal of porpoises. They are very large fish, being from four to six feet in length. They can swim very fast, and they kept well in front of the Chimborazo. For more than an hour swimming just below the surface of the water, and now and then taking a jump clear out of the water. On this day we kept closer to the shore. The coast is very rocky and wild looking but very picturesque. A long way inland, we could all see the mountains rising to a tremendous height, but we were not near enough to see them nicely. About 11:30am we had a slight delay caused by the carelessness of one of the engineers, but in about an hour and a half we resumed our voyage. Towards evening we drew so far from land that we lost sight of it altogether. Several whales were seen, but not too close to the ship.

Wednesday 25th April 1883

When I went upon deck this morning, I was much disappointed by the discovery that we had passed Gibraltar during the night. I was very desirous of having a look at the forts, being the strongest England possessed. But I missed it. One of the sailors informed me that he himself had never seen it and yet he had passed it many times, but always at night. We were now not far off the south coast of Spain, and we could see the mountains known as Sierra Nevada. This was a pretty sight indeed or rather a grand sight. The peaks rise very high but we could see no sign of habitation or cultivation upon them, look where we would, it was mountains, rough, rugged and wild.

We passed about forty vessels during the day, chiefly sailing vessels, and although they had a great spread of canvas, they scarcely seemed to move, for the air was as still as could be, and the sea quite calm. In the evening we saw sharks, but like the whales they were a good distance off. All kinds of games were carried on now while the ship was going so smoothly. Jumping, leap frog, cards, dancing and even cricket on a small scale, and in fact, anything and everything that could be thought of or invented in the way of games. When night closed in singing on deck was resorted to. This was very pleasant, as evenings were growing warmer, for we were getting towards Italy.

I now had a good chance of seeing all my fellow passengers, and I found we were a mixed party altogether. We had one or two Frenchmen, two Germans, one Italian, numbers of Scotch and Irish, fourteen Welshmen, and one or two whose nationality I did not discover. The different religious denominations were well represented too. There were two or three R.C. priests, and several Sisters of Mercy, a Church of England clergyman and one or two of almost every denomination in existence.

Thursday 26th April 1883

The amusements I have before mentioned continued to attract the passengers until today; the weather having been fine since the 25th April. But this evening about 8 o'clock, the wind rose considerably, and the water even began to wash the decks occasionally. We expected a rough night and we had it too. I was awakened about 12 o'clock by the noise of the wind and waves, which were like thunder. I could hear wave after wave strike against the sides of the ship, and the water washed across the deck and down the hatchways and into every place that was not quickly covered up. The sailors had a very lively time at first, as the hatchways had to be covered with tarpaulins, properly secured to prevent the wind from blowing it, or the waves from washing it away.

To add to the general confusion a good number of passengers were up and down the greater part of the night through seasickness, and of course they got a soaking with salt water as soon as they stepped upon deck. I lay and listened to all this for a long time but at last I dropped off to sleep. I did not wake again until daylight, when I myself had a severe attack of seasickness, and I went to bed again very quickly and remained there until about 4 o'clock in the afternoon, when I felt a little better. But the ship was rolling and pitching in all directions. One minute we were riding on the top of a huge wave, and the next we plunged down into a deep valley, from which it seemed impossible to rise. Of course this was all very well for those that could appreciate it, but it caused us landsmen to have some very unpleasant sensations. Throughout the day, one or other of the passengers kept giving way to their feelings in the usual way, but by bedtime the sea went down considerably, and there was the prospect of a fine day on the morrow.

Saturday 28th April 1883

Fine weather and smooth sea once more. We were now getting very near Naples at which place we expected to go ashore. In the morning we passed a number of small islands, very beautiful to look at. Some of them were spotted with trees, houses and gardens. The houses have a very pretty appearance when looked at from the sea being built of a light coloured stone, or painted white. As we entered the Bay of Naples, the scenery was more lovely than ever. The Bay is in the form of a half circle, or perhaps more like a horseshoe, and the houses and other buildings extended above half way around, the greater part being on the left side as you enter from the sea. Farther back the houses are upon high rocks, and surrounded by fruit trees and gardens.

On the other side of the bay, the volcano Vesuvius rises high above everything. The sides of it are all black and dirty looking and covered with lava, the deposit of eruptions in years gone by. From the crater a cloud of smoke is continually hissing, as if to remind us of the mighty power that lies hidden in the depths. Around the base is a small village, and we saw one or two houses built almost half way up the mountain. How any sane person can live there is more than I can understand. Surely they must forget that such a place as the city of Pompeii ever existed and was buried by the eruption of the same mountain, upon whose sides they have built their homes. But we are now past the breakwater and the anchor is down and we have plenty of time to look about.

Many small boats crowded around us, the owners having all sorts of articles for sale. Straw hats, baskets, coral, breads, jewellery, fruit etc. At last a small tender came along to fetch us ashore, for which we had to pay the modest sum of 2/6 each. I say modest as it took us nearly five minutes to get the landing place. But who cares so that we can set foot on terra firma once more. By the time we landed it was 4 o'clock, so we had to make the most of our time, which was very limited. The first thing I did was to join a party and engage a guide, as without one we could scarcely do anything. We first strolled round a few of the principal streets. They are very narrow, and not any too clean, but some of the houses are very fine structures, varying from three to six floors high.

The streets are crowded with all sorts of vehicles but the horses drawing them are very small, and are being badly fed and badly cared for, or so it seemed to me. After spending a little time in this way we visited one or two Roman Catholic churches. The workmanship displayed inside these places is something wonderful. The floors are made of marble, not plain slabs, but in small pieces of all colours, and laid in all kinds of beautiful patterns and designs. The walls are gilded, covered with images, and statues of the Virgin Mary, Our Saviour and many saints, with whose names I am not acquainted. The ceilings are beautifully painted in pictures by the most eminent artists Italy could produce. On either side are some beautifully carved confessional boxes. In one of them sat a priest and on both sides of the box is a small door. To one of these he placed his ear, while a lady outside, kneeling on the floor, was confessing her sins to him, instead of carrying her troubles to her maker. Other women were kneeling before their patron saints, telling their beads and going through other forms of religion.

Having spent a considerable time in the churches we next visited a burying place, belonging to some distinguished family. It was built in the form of a large room, something like a chapel, the floor being covered with marble figures, each one representing some member of the family buried there some time during the past two centuries. This ceiling was also painted in a beautiful manner. We next visited a few of the poorer streets. Here, the front rooms of the houses are used as workshops, sleeping apartments, and roosting places for fowls, some of them being used for all these purposes at once. It now began to get dark, and we thought it wise to return to the Chimborazo, and so we discharged our guide and returned by way of the markets, purchasing some beautiful figs and oranges on our way. After getting on board, we found it was a very pretty sight to look across the water and see the city by night. Most of the houses contained a light, and as they are built very close together it looked something like an illumination. About 10 o'clock it began to rain heavily, and we were very glad to get below and rest ourselves, leaving the sailors to take in the remainder of the cargo, and prepare for another start.

Sunday 29th April 1883

We left Naples at midnight, and by the time I awoke, the city was a long way behind us. About 2 o'clock in the afternoon we entered the Straits of Messina. On our right lay the island of Sicily, on our left we could see the south coast of Italy. The straits are very narrow and we were about two hours going through. The scenery on the coast of Italy is magnificent, and the sun was shining full upon it, but the island was so much in the shade that we could distinguish very little. The south of Italy is very mountainous and rocky, but beautiful. At the front of the nearest hills or mountains nestled small towns and villages and the beach was strewn with fishing smacks and other small craft. The sides of the lowest and most gradually sloping mountains appeared to be laid out in gardens, vineyards, and clusters of orange and fig trees and could be plainly seen. Here and there are patches of rocks, barren and bare. A railway runs along the coast not far inland, and we could see a train as it steamed along over the bridges that were built across rivers that came pouring down from the distant mountains, the tops of which were covered with snow all year round. However, we gradually lost sight of it all, and by 6 o'clock we were out of sight of everything except water, and making way under sail and steam for Port Said in Egypt, our next stopping place.

Wednesday 2nd May 1883

We arrived at Port Said at 4 pm after a very pleasant voyage from Naples. The sun had been very hot for a day or two, and the wind quiet, but there was a very heavy swelling on the water, and we shipped some heavy seas once or twice, but nothing occurred worthy of note. As soon as we dropped anchor we were again surrounded by small boats containing tobacco, tea and fruit, which the owners offered for sale. Some were waiting to take passengers ashore, and in this respect, we were treated a little better than at Naples, as we were only asked to pay six pence.

No sooner were we landed than we were besieged by guides and beggars, the former offering their services, the latter asking for mannish or baksheesh. This time however we did not require a guide, as the place is not nearly so large as Naples. The main street starts near the wharf and runs straight through the town. We went through this first and then turned into another street, where a kind of market was held. This was a very dirty street, but it was hard to say which was the more dirty, the streets or the inhabitants. There were stalls containing all kinds of eatables, such as fruit, biscuits and some dirty looking cakes, also a few vegetables, the whole being a motley collection, not at all tempting to Europeans in general, and Englishmen in particular. The largest shops were those situated near the water, and some of them were kept by Englishmen.

After looking over the centre of town, we took a stroll around the outskirts, during which we came across a place of worship, or mosque I think they call it. It was used by Arabs. As they entered, each man took off his sandals and left them just outside the door, walked inside, and knelt down, placing his hands upon the ground, and their faces in their hands, and in this attitude they went through their evening devotions. There were only about half a dozen there, when we peered in, but of course we were not allowed to enter, being of a different religion.

We now began to get rather tired as the streets were mostly covered with sand, making it rather hard walking. On our way back we had a short conversation with a young Egyptian who could speak a little English, and he told us that one English soldier was worth ten of his countrymen, showing that they have a very great respect for our army. Some of the hotels in Port Said are very attractive; we entered one, and the room in which we found ourselves was large enough to dine several hundred persons. At one end, upon a platform, was a string band. About a dozen females were playing violins, and besides these were a few men, playing bass viola, and violincellos, etc. They played some splendid music too, so that I could not help staying a while to listen. About the room were placed tables of various sizes and shapes, some of them with marble tops, and chairs were scattered about the room in all directions. In fact, a regular free and easy sort of place. I need scarcely say they attracted a great deal of custom, especially from visitors coming from the steamboats, that were daily calling there for coal, or for other purposes.

We could not stay here long as it was now getting late, and after looking at one or two more places of interest we returned to the Chimborazo. It was now about 10 o'clock. There we found everything in a perfect muddle. Everything was dirty and smothered in coal dust, they having shipped a supply of coal to carry us the remainder of the journey. This was brought to the ship's side in barges, or lighters, or whatever they are called. Two planks were then placed from them on to the ship, and the coal was carried in baskets by the natives, who were bare footed, and in a few hours they had carried about six hundred tons.

Thursday 3rd May 1883

At 6 o'clock in the morning we left Port Said, and entered the Suez Canal. It is about 50 or 60 yards wide, but only in the centre is it deep enough for a large vessel to travel with safety. We found this part of the journey very tedious; no vessel of any size is allowed to travel more than four or five miles per hour. Twice during the day we had to stop and draw to one side to allow others to pass in an opposite direction, as there is not enough room for two to pass, only at certain places widened out on purpose, and even then one must stop. This occupied about an hour and a half each time, so we made very slow progress. At twenty minutes past seven it began to get dark, and as no ship is allowed to travel in the canal at night, the anchor was dropped, and we were at a standstill, after steaming only 30 miles.

Friday 4th May 1883

We started again at 6:30 am after waiting for two others to pass. The heat at midday was very great (about 90 degrees in the shade) and we had nothing on either side but hot, sandy plains. We passed Ismalia, where Garnet Wolseley landed most of the English troops ready for the late war. We also saw the building he used as a hospital afterwards for the wounded soldiers. Several times we had to lay to for others to pass, and in the afternoon we had to wait for no less than four in rotation. The first of these turned and came gently towards us. Our first officer shouted to the man at the wheel, telling him to keep clear, but it was afterwards found that the steering went wrong, just at the particular moment, so that the man had no power. On it came and ran into the Chimborazo, giving us a tremendous shaking from stem to stern.

The headboard was smashed, and the port anchor fastenings cut in two, and down went the anchor with a splash, into the water. Many of the women began to cry, thinking no doubt we were about to be drowned, but as we were only about 30 ft from terra firma, there was not much danger of that. By the time the remaining three had passed, it was time for us to stop for the night, so of course we just remained where we were. Many of the passengers put on bathing dresses and had a good swim in the canal, which I have no doubt was very refreshing after the heat of the day. By the way, this day was my 21st birthday, and the first I had spent away from home.

Saturday 5th May 1883

In the morning we had to wait again for others to pass, amongst them the English troop ship, Crocodile, with several hundred soldiers on board, homeward bound from India. At last we arrived at Suez about 9:30am, and were done with the canal. After a slight delay we entered the Red Sea and were once more bowling along at twelve to fourteen knots an hour. It was very pleasant to see the waves once more, and to feel the motion of the vessel, after being in the canal for about 51 hours, and only travelling 93 miles. We could see land on either side, the African coast on the starboard and the Arabian coast on the port side. Both shores appeared very rocky and bare, but that did not make it less interesting. The heat was so intense now that we had more sea room. We could feel a nice breeze coming from ahead, which was much better than the land breezes in the canal, for they tasted too much of the hot sandy deserts of Africa that extended farther than we could see.

Sunday 6th May 1883

The sea was smoother on this day than on any day during the whole voyage, it looked just like a sheet of glass, and was as still as a mill pond. In the morning I attended the Protestant service on the quarterdeck, and another service of the same kind was held in the afternoon in the second saloons. The saloon was occupied in the morning by Roman Catholics, of whom we had a goodly number on board, mostly Irish. The evening we spent lounging about the deck, having nothing better to do. The next day (Monday) was very hot, but we still had a head wind, so that made it a little better. We saw numbers of flying fish now, for the first time.

Wednesday 7th May 1883

The weather now began to get hotter every day, so instead of sleeping below I carried my bed upstairs, and slept on deck all night, and found it much cooler. I found it rather inconvenient in the morning as the decks had to be washed down at about 4 o'clock, but I was repaid for my early rising by watching the sunrise, which is a very beautiful sight. We now passed some very curious rocks, which were projecting out of the water. There are twelve of them, and they are called the twelve apostles. Somewhere near these rocks, we saw no less than three wrecks, the Pelican, Duke of Lancaster and the Gulf of Finland.

In the evening we witnessed a very beautiful sunset, such as not to be seen in England. The sky seemed all on fire at first and then gradually changed to a golden hue, and then there were streaks of green and blue and almost every other colour, and at last the sun seemed to sink right into the sea, and in a very short time it became quite dark.

Thursday 10th May 1883

During the night we came through what are commonly known as Hell's Gates. This, I think, is a rather dangerous place near some rocks, but as I was asleep at the time, I cannot describe it. We passed Aden very early in the morning, so I did not see that either. We were now out of the Red Sea, and into the Ocean. At 8 o'clock a little child was buried. It had been suffering from bronchitis, and died this morning at 5 o'clock, and was at once sewn in a piece of new sail cloth, with a bar of iron on each side of it. The ship was brought to, and a short service was read and then at a given signal, the body was dropped overboard by two sailors. Just one splash and all was over, and in a few minutes it was left far behind us.

Friday 11th May 1883

The heat today seemed greater than ever, and to add to our discomfort, the water we had to drink was quite warm. We were now making for the island of Diego Garcia. We had just three weeks at sea, and had done the most pleasant part of the voyage, though not the longest part. We now had a little rough weather, and of course I was ill once again. I was not sea sick, but I had a very severe headache, and was altogether out of sorts. From the 11th to the 14th (Whit Monday) I could only eat one meal, and this was brought to me on deck by a shipmate named Charles Davies, with whom I had formed a friendship. I now stayed on deck day and night, as I felt better there than down below. In the daytime I had my blanket and pillow to lie upon, and at night my other things were brought to me.

Friday 18th May 1883

The past week has seemed very long to me. Nothing but headaches and other bad feelings. I continued living upon nothing, until I almost got used to it. We arrived at Diego Garcia on the 17th and as soon as the vessel got into smooth water, I felt better at once. We stayed until 11.30 pm today, and then made another start, and it was not many hours before my old complaint returned to me again.

During the last day or two we had some very heavy rain. Not rain as we are used to in England, but real downpours, such as only to be experienced in tropical Diego Garcia. The few little islands near it are situated in one of the most rainy parts of the Indian Ocean, and I am told they get rain about seven or eight months out of twelve. The soil is very fertile, and the islands are covered with coconut palms and other trees and shrubs. There are only a few dwellings on the place, and these are to accommodate the agents of different shipping companies, whose vessels call here for coal. We landed one passenger here, a diver, who came on board at Naples. He had been engaged by the Orient Company to assist in raising the SS Austral, a large vessel that sank in Sydney harbour some time ago. He was now on his way home, but having arrived as far as Naples, he received a telegram to say he was to return as far as Diego Garcia on some new business. He therefore took a passage on the

Chimborazo, being the first boat that came since he received his orders.

For about twelve days after leaving the island, our journey was very monotonous, nothing to see but water day after day, and the weather mostly rough, as we had winds all the time. The top masts had to be taken down to prevent the ship being top heavy, as she might have tipped over and not righted herself. Upon one occasion, she rolled so that the sail was only two or three feet out of the water; when in smooth water this same sail would be about 18ft out of the water. We shipped some very heavy seas sometimes, which of course wetted anyone to the skin who was unfortunate enough to be standing in the way.

Sunday 22nd May 1883

A flying fish was caught. It was about the size and shape of an English mackerel with wings about six inches long. They are to be seen in large numbers in the Indian Ocean.

Tuesday 24th May 1883

Today was the Queen's birthday. This event does not pass unnoticed at sea, but is marked by an unlimited supply of plum pudding, or plum duff, as it is generally called on board ship. At this time we had very heavy cross seas, which caused the vessel to roll to such an extent that boxes, water cans etc., went sliding across the floor, first to one side and then back again to the other. This continued at intervals for two or three days, disturbing us very much at night, and sometimes in the day time, throwing nearly everything off the table, as we sat at breakfast or dinner. I had quite recovered my usual health by this time, and although the sea was very rough, I did not feel at all bad. I suppose I was getting used to it.

Sunday 29th May 1883

It has been a very cold, wet and altogether miserable day. The rain was very heavy indeed. On the 30th about 9 o'clock in the morning, two or three waterspouts were seen a short distance from the boat, but unfortunately I was below at the time so I missed the sight.

Memories of Houghton Regis

Saturday 2nd June 1883

At about noon, we passed Cape Otway. This was the first sight of land for fourteen days, but we lost sight of it again, until Sunday morning at 4 o'clock. At five a pilot came aboard to take us up to the wharf at Williamstown, where we arrived at half past ten. The Chimborazo was soon made fast, so that we could go ashore and return as often as we pleased. We were not slow to avail ourselves of this opportunity.

In the morning I went for a short walk with one or two others, and after dinner we went down by the beach, and gathered seaweed and shells. Returning to the wharf, we went over to one of the P&O Company's mail boats, which was lying on the opposite side of the wharf. Some of our fellow passengers had found friends waiting for them; others had gone by train to Melbourne to spend the day, so that when we returned to tea, the tables were almost deserted. During the day, I had not walked more than three miles, and yet I felt as tired and as stiff as I should in walking twenty, at any other time. On Monday I arose in good time, and found the crew busy unshipping the Melbourne baggage and cargo, and after seeing that my own was safe, I took a train to Melbourne with my friend Charley Davis.

Melbourne seems to be a very nice place, the streets are wide, and the buildings handsome, but they are very low compared with the buildings in London, none of them running more than three storeys. The Post Office and the banks are built of stone and are very fine looking buildings. After taking dinner we visited the arcades in Bourke Street where we saw the most beautiful articles for sale. We also visited the Museum, Library and Picture Gallery, which are all in one building in Swanston Street. Looking at it from the street, the building looks very much like the British Museum, but it is not like it much inside. The statuary was not of the best, but just passable. In the first two rooms we entered, we saw articles from all parts of the world. Clubs and spears from Fiji, Ashanti, Zululand and the South Sea Islands. There were native dresses, ornaments, canoes etc., also guns, swords, pistols and other weapons, relics of the Indian mutiny.

In another room we saw models of all kinds of machinery, made as perfect as possible. Ploughs, threshing machines and other farming implements, also railway engines, silk looms and weaving machinery. In another room, we found samples of wood and minerals and other things from various places. In fact, there seemed to be a bit of everything from every land. There were specimens of woodcarvings and model houses and palaces. In a large glass case was a model of one of Her Majesty's ships of war, mounted with brass cannons. In another case, a model of the SS Orient, the largest of the Orient fleet. This was a splendid piece of workmanship. Not a rope, block or piece of chain was missing. All the windlasses and other pieces of machinery about the deck were made in brass. Not a single thing was left out. We saw many other interesting sights here, and then we went through the library and picture gallery. We then went out, and after purchasing a very good tea, we returned to Williamstown and arrived on board about half past nine thoroughly tired out, so that we could scarcely get into bed. However, a good night's rest, without the usual rocking of the vessel put us to rights again, and as we did not expect to start before 3 o'clock, we went and had a final look around Williamstown, returning at twelve to dinner.

At 3 o'clock the ship's bell rang to tell visitors to leave the ship, and in a short time the captain gave word to let go the fastenings, and the good old ship began to move slowly from the wharf. Just at this moment half a dozen men were seen running along the wharf having stayed on shore a trifle too long. But the Chimborazo was three or four feet from the wharf, and the companion ladder was drawn in by the time they arrived. A rope was thrown out, and one man managed to grasp it and scrambled on board. Fortunately, a party of workmen were passing in a boat and the five that were left got in, and were rowed alongside, before she had got a fair start. The distance was only thirty yards, but they had to pay ten shillings for it. A rope ladder was thrown out by the sailors, and they all managed to scramble aboard, but no effort was made by the Captain or officers to assist them. By the time it was dark, we were about forty miles from Melbourne, and going along with fair winds and fair weather, at about ten knots an hour.

We had what the sailors called an unusually good passage round the coast for the time of year, as it is usually rough. The sea was very quiet, and the sun shone brightly all the way, and as we were not more than three or four miles from shore, it was a very pleasant journey.

Memories of Houghton Regis

Thursday 7th June 1883

At 3 o'clock we passed the heads, and entered Sydney harbour, which is a beautiful one, and is said to be one of the prettiest harbours in the world. About 4 o'clock we dropped anchor in Neutral Bay, and I lost no time in bidding goodbye to the Chimborazo, and the storms, and pleasures and dangers of a long sea voyage.

Altogether, we did not do as badly as we might have done, as the Chimborazo had been twice partially wrecked, once in the Bay of Biscay in a storm and once through running straight upon a rock between Melbourne and Sydney. This rock was pointed out to us by the sailors, but we were too far off to run upon it this time. We stepped on shore at the Circular Quay at 5 o' clock, and I for one was very thankful that we had arrived safely. The journey from Tilbury to Sydney had taken exactly seven weeks to accomplish.

George Tompkins (right). Taken in Sydney mid-late 1880s (GT)

Walter Barrett and his wife in Australia, around 1899 (GT)

Cement Manufacture in Houghton Regis

From information supplied by David Simms and Dr Chris Downs, from Lafarge Cement UK Plc

Background

Bedfordshire was a late entrant into modern large-scale cement manufacture. Although geologically the southern half of the county is well provided with the necessary raw materials (chalk and clay), there were few large urban market areas until the late nineteenth century. Communication (road, rail or canal) along the base of the chalk scarp where the raw materials were most accessible was generally poor, thus hindering effective distribution.

Rail access along the foot of the chalk scarp was achieved in two stages when railway lines were opened from Leighton Buzzard and Luton to Houghton Regis in 1848 and 1858. However, to judge by the First Edition Ordnance Survey Map of 1879, neither railway had stimulated any significant quarry development by then.

Several limeworks developed in the scarp, mostly on a small scale, including Sewell, Sundon, Totternhoe and Blows Down. Because the specific needs of the lime kiln technology of the nineteenth century was for large lumps of chalk, small chalk accumulated as a waste product.

One or two limeworks – Totternhoe most notably - became involved indirectly in the cement industry, but in Warwickshire, not Bedfordshire. Because Warwickshire limestone is mostly of poor quality, cement could only be made from it by adding a proportion of higher quality chalk. Thus, Totternhoe began to send waste small chalk (but still of high chemical quality) by rail to the Rugby and Southern cement works in Warwickshire. Bedfordshire still supplies high-grade chalk to Rugby, from Kensworth, but via pipeline, not rail.

The first successful cement works in Bedfordshire is thought to have been at Arlesey near Hitchin in 1883, which was followed in 1899 by one at Sundon. But trading conditions deteriorated around the turn of the century due to excess capacity, low demand and antiquated processes, largely based upon modifications of lime kiln technology.

At that period, the rotary kiln made its first appearances in the UK, resulting in a dramatic improvement in productivity and quality, but also requiring greatly increased capital investment and, hence, a step change in the plant capacity.

Coping with all these challenges proved too much for the old industry. A series of amalgamations occurred, the most notable being the formation of Associated Portland Cement Manufacturers (1900) Ltd in that year, and its subsidiary company British Portland Cement Manufacturers Ltd in 1911. From then on, small older works were closed and production concentrated on fewer, larger works modernised with rotary kilns. In Bedfordshire, Arlesey works came into the APCM fold in 1900 and Sundon into BPCM in 1912. Lafarge is the current successor (owner) since 2001.

History of the Houghton Regis Cement Works

APCM (colloquially 'the combine') and BPCM dominated UK cement supply; the extent of that dominance prompted entrepreneurs to challenge it by constructing an all-new cement works based upon the latest technologies. It was those challenges that led to the development of the Houghton Regis cement works in 1925-26 by the Portland Cement Company Ltd., constructed by engineers Maxted & Knott. This completely new works had an initial capacity of about 110,000 tons per annum of cement, produced from two rotary kilns.

However, the new plant, like a number of others in southern England which had also been built with the intention of outflanking APCM/BPCM, opened in the midst of the economic depression, and almost immediately found itself in financial difficulties. Accordingly, Houghton Regis and others formed themselves into a third combine, the Red Triangle Group, in 1927. The formation of this group failed to cure their economic difficulties and, on 30th October 1931, it collapsed, Houghton Regis and other works being acquired by APCM.

As economic conditions improved, the Houghton Regis works

Memories of Houghton Regis

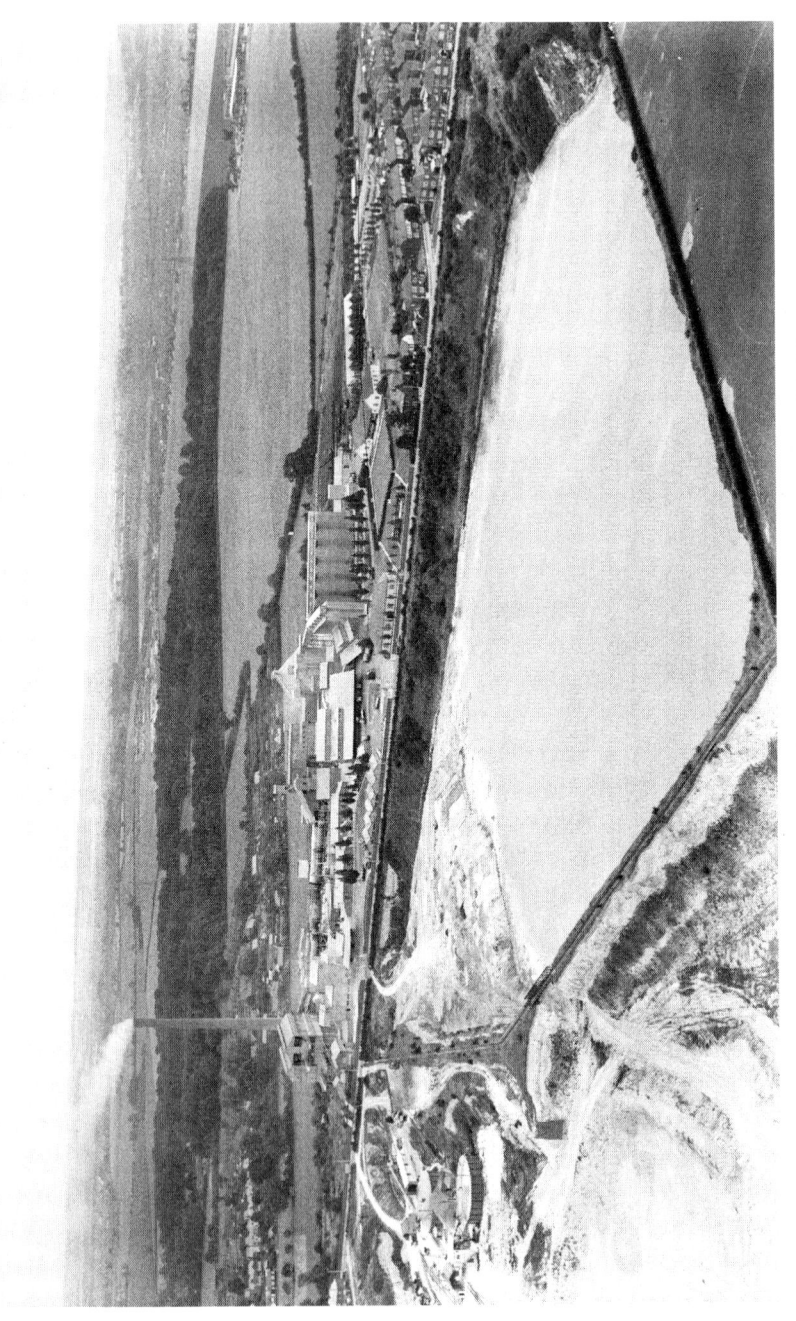

Houghton Regis Cement Works Aerial View, 1961 (DG/LM)

developed further – a third kiln was added in 1936, and the first kiln modernised in 1943 so that, by the 1950s, capacity was up to about 320,000 tons per annum, where it remained. In addition to cement, the works also produced hydrated lime under the trade name 'Hydralime'. This was the result of APCM deciding to close its old local limeworks (Sewell and Blows Down) and replace them with brand new plant in the cement works curtilage.

Prior to the 1931 takeover, employees, skilled and unskilled throughout the country must have been attracted to work at the Houghton plant. Some employees were transferred from the APCM Peters Cement Works, south of Rochester, Kent, which closed around 1925. Other staff transferred from the various limeworks that had closed around Dunstable.

By the 1960s, the cement industry was over its post war boom and in need of further modernisation and rationalisation. In the south of England, this manifested itself in the construction of the world's largest wet-process cements works, at Northfleet on the Kent bank of the river Thames, which opened in 1969/70. With a design capacity of 3.6 million tons of cement (ten times the size of the Houghton plant), it was intended to replace a dozen small and ageing works.

Houghton Regis was one of the victims of this centralisation, ceasing to manufacture cement on 31st March 1971. It was retained as a depot to redistribute cement brought in by rail from elsewhere until July 1978, after which the site was demolished and redeveloped.

Although the closure was precipitated by the new Northfleet works, Houghton Regis could not have continued in operation much longer in any event. Its quarry was running out of chalk, and the proximity of the main A5 and housing, plus downland of high amenity value, would have caused great difficulties to any attempt to extend the quarry.

Processes and employment

The quarry was located immediately west of the cement works, separated from it by Houghton Road. Chalk and marl were quarried by face shovel, loaded into railway wagons and hauled to washmills near the Houghton Road. Here the minerals were blended with water to make chalk and marl slurries, which were then piped under the road to the works to be blended in their optimum proportions.

Memories of Houghton Regis

Last of the Cement Works. The 400 ft chimney with its vanquisher Ron Ransford 1978 (DG/LM)

Cement Manufacture in Houghton Regis

Memories of Houghton Regis

Steam locomotives were used originally, but internal combustion locomotives were early competitors; indeed, the very first locomotive, new in 1925, was petrol rather than steam, and the last steamers left in 1967.

In October 1963, the quarry was being worked in two levels or 'benches'. The upper bench won higher-grade chalk, while the lower bench won the clayey chalk marl. The remaining life of the quarry was then estimated at only 4 1/2 years at the full rated production of 326,000 tons per annum of cement clinker, or 6 years, if the blend of high/low grade materials was altered. Hence, the works was at the natural end of its life when closed in 1971.

Although the quarry had some novel features, the process of cement making was very much the standard 'wet process', so called because it involves blending the chalk and clay as slurries, and as distinct from the 'dry process', where the materials are blended without adding extra water.

From the washmills, the blended slurry was pumped into the upper (cooler) ends of the rotary kilns. Inside each kiln was a rotating steel tube, lined with firebrick, at a slight angle to the horizontal. The kilns were probably some 10-12ft diameter and 300 ft long.

Thus, as the slurry passed down the kiln its temperature was raised. At the top end, the temperature might be only about 150-200°C and the effect of the heat was mainly to dry off the water. Nearing the lower end of the kiln, temperatures would increase to around 1,300°C and the chemical constituents of the chalk and clay would be combined to form cement clinker. Exhaust gases would pass, via electrostatic precipitators (to remove dust) to the 400 ft high chimney.

The clinker would then fall out of the kiln into a cooler (blowing air through it), before passing on to storage. When required, the clinker would be passed from the clinker store to grinding mills where it would be reduced from hard nodulised lumps to the familiar fine grey powder. At this stage, a small percentage of gypsum would be added (3-5%) to stop the cement setting too quickly and, depending upon the type of cement being made, perhaps other minor additives as well.

The final cement would be stored in bulk silos for onward transport by road or rail tankers, or sent to the bagging plant for sale in 1-cwt bags.

An enormous variety of jobs existed at the plant. Excavating, driving locomotives, tipping the rail waggons, operating the washmills, pumping the slurry, controlling ("burning") the kiln, operating grinding mills and the various conveyors connecting each part of the process. Loading lorries and rail wagons with bulk or bagged cement, receiving coal and other stores – all required their different specialisms. Then there were the various services; electrical, mechanical and motor engineering – to keep the plant running, plus the works chemist to ensure the product was of the right quality. Above those were the various managerial functions – quarry, plant, sales, personnel, etc., with their clerical assistants, and, at the top of the pyramid, the Works Manager. Records show that the plant probably employed around 200 people at the peak of its production.

An in-house journal was produced for the employees – called The Blue Circle. In the July 1952 edition the following article appeared:

"The welfare side of the works has always been a feature right from the early years, but in 1951 it received a great boost, when the new canteen, social club, bowls green and tennis courts were opened by our Chairman, Mr G F Earle. Now, under energetic sport and entertainments committees, events follow each other in rapid succession. In the local Darts League, it seems strange to see "A.P.C.M" lying third amidst a welter of "Greyhounds", "Red Lions" and "Pheasants"! It is of interest to note that there are now no less than seven sports sub committees.

"We hesitate to hark back to the war years, but those who served will ever remember the kindly thought that prompted the H.M.F. Fund. Every employee contributed 6d per week to this fund, which enabled the Welfare Committee to distribute around £250 each year in the shape of parcels of books, cigarettes and Christmas boxes to all serving men. The wives and children left behind were also cared for in times of sickness and received a very welcome Christmas box each year. A chatty little circular was published regularly and sent out to all men in the forces, and when they came back they received a gift of £5."

Postscript –
"In 1954, work commenced on the erection of a motor repair depot at the works. It came into commission in the early part of 1955, and is now the base for major repairs and overhauls for the lorries of the Midland Area."

Cement Manufacture in Houghton Regis

Workers from the Cement Plant in Houghton Regis listen to a health and safety message, 1952 (DG)

Memories of Houghton Regis

Employees at the cement works queue to receive money from the company's profit sharing scheme in 1954 (DG)

Mr & Mrs Cherry

Mrs Cherry - My twin sister and I were born in this house in 1933. The cement company built these houses in Mill Road and in Townsend Terrace for their workers in 1927, so everybody knew everyone else. We all used to play together; it was like one big family. I left home when I got married and came back and bought this house in 1972, when the cement works sold it.

My grandfather was a steel worker but as there was very little work up North he found a job here, building all the gantries for the cement plant. My father was the quarry foreman and he was later joined by all three of my brothers, who when old enough, worked there as well.

They enjoyed working there, although the cement dust caused a lot of controversy. We were sort of brought up on it and I don't think we did too badly! All the hedges and roads were covered in dust, but we had no reason to complain because after all, it was our bread and butter. They used to dump all the chalk rubbish at the top where the fields were and, when the wind blew this way, the dust covered our houses until they started to use sprinklers. Eventually Readymix set up on the other side of Millers Way – that's where all the wash mills and grinders for the cement works were. Some of them are still buried underneath there, I think.

Mr Cherry – They had a gantry over the road where they used to take chalk across on two-way buckets. The main buildings and kilns were on one side of the road and the pits were on the other. There also used to be a railway line that went into the back of the cement plant. It was a twenty-four hour operation. They were quarrying all day and night.

Mrs Cherry - You got used to the noise, in fact the only time my Dad used to wake up at night was when the machines stopped, and he used to know that there had been a breakdown. My brothers followed my father into quarry work. My middle brother was a chemist there before he went to war, and my youngest brother was in charge of lorry maintenance.

When the cement plant shut down many people were very concerned about the loss of jobs. My mum was still living in this house when the company decided to sell all their properties. At that time she was in poor health and the family got together and suggested that we buy the house; they were sold off cheaper to the tenants. We purchased it in 1972, looked after Mum until she died in 1981, and here we stayed.

Members of the Baptist Church gather after a successful church fete, in the shadow of the cement works, c 1956 (DG)

A New Life...

So many people have moved to Houghton Regis and made it their home. On the whole, it was the result of finding employment. The railway, the cement company and later on, expanding manufacturing industries, of which Vauxhall is probably the best known, have attracted people from all over the country.

The major industrial and manufacturing industries of the 1950s, 60s and 70s, and the need to create homes for vast numbers of people were the catalysts for building the Tithe Farm and Parkside Estates in the town. Desperately overcrowded and in some cases, incredibly expensive, people found it exceptionally hard to find somewhere to live in London. Not only did these estates provide good, sizeable houses for families unable to find accommodation in the capital, but they represented a whole new way of life.

Set against a backdrop of rural England, many people described their new homes as 'wonderful', modern and spacious. They loved Houghton Regis, the countryside, made new friends and happily settled into the town. However, some of the first residents found that the pavements and roads were not yet completed, and schools and other amenities were yet to be built. A number of local entrepreneurs stepped in to help with this situation, by selling their goods from mobile vans or shops! Other people missed their families and the lives they had in London, and decided to return. Moving away from friends and family, changing jobs and adopting a new lifestyle could not have been easy, but many people have done just that – these are their stories…

Pat Lovering

I came to Houghton Regis with my two young sons to join my husband Peter at the end of 1964. He was to open the new Youth Club in Bedford Square, having recently qualified as a Youth Leader.

At this time, the 14th century Tithe Barn and the old Tithe Farmhouse had been demolished to make way for Bedford Square, (duly opened by Hattie Jacques in 1966), but the rest of the village was intact.

The Blue Circle Cement Works was situated in the High Street, and my children were fascinated by the white roofs of the houses all around. They thought it must be snow, and were quite disappointed to be told it was just dust…the dust was very pervasive – we lived quite a way from the centre of the village, but the furniture was always dusted with a light layer of white soon after you had cleaned.

We loved all the little shops in the High Street. There were two or three bakers, butchers who hung their own meat, little general stores, sweet shops and pretty cottages along the High Street. Although the buildings were largely brick faced at the front, many of them were traditionally built with timber beams and brick infill, or white wattle-and-daub at the back. (You can see this at Regents Motors today. The only place in the High Street – apart from All Saints Church.)

The children particularly liked going to Jasper Perry's shop opposite Tithe Farm Road. What attracted Bradley and Peter was the 'sixpenny drawer'. The shop was fitted out in the old fashioned way with a long counter on one side with shelves and drawers along the other wall. These drawers were quite deep and in one of them was a selection of small toys, any of which could be had for sixpence each. The boys used to race down the road with their pocket money on Saturdays and the excitement was intense!

I used to like going to Sonny Pratt's butcher's shop, to the little baker in Queen Street run by Percy Ward, and to have a chat with Mrs Dunham in the Wool Shop, where I bought the children's clothes.

Soon, however, the dead hand of the Compulsory Purchase Orders took effect, and slowly the shops and houses lost heart and the owners moved out. I think the official view was that the shops would move into Bedford Square. Mrs Durham did indeed move there, but the rent and rates were unsustainable and she had to close the shop, and I cannot remember anyone else trying.

To my horror the bulldozers and wrecking balls moved slowly up the High Street demolishing the old Five Bells pub, the homes, the shops and, in a fundamental way, the village.

At the time, I didn't think that Houghton Regis would survive this

A New Life...

wholesale demolition and wave after wave of overspill development. But it has not only survived, but transformed itself into a town, and a busy one at that!

Members of the Houghton Regis Youth Centre, 1967 (DG/LM)

Betty Grayson

It was around 1946, after the end of the war, and it was very difficult to find anywhere to live, so I got a job as housekeeper at the White House in Houghton Regis. It was very funny really – I didn't even know how to boil an egg! I'd been a real spoilt darling at home and never lifted a finger! Also, by that time I was married and pregnant with my daughter, so for the first year of working there, I had a cookery book in one hand and a baby under the other arm! Captain Howard Smith lived there at the time - he was from an army family and seemed very posh to me, but he was a very, very nice person. We got on extremely well; there was none of this upstairs, downstairs business. He needed a housekeeper because his wife had died after her third baby was born. He also had two other girls who went to boarding school. However, there was one thing that he was very snooty about. I had joined the Women's Institute and I think we met about once a fortnight, so on those particular evenings, instead of cooking a proper meal, I'd get fish and chips, but he absolutely refused to eat it. I think he thought they were rather vulgar, so he used to boil himself an egg!

It was a very old but beautiful house with a huge garden. The ceilings had the most enormous oak beams, and the floors on the ground floor were made of bricks that a cleaning lady used to polish every week. On the upper floors it had very uneven but polished wooden floorboards.

We lived in part of the house, with two bedrooms and a sitting room. This was a small room with flowers from the creepers outside hanging over the windows - very pretty. My husband used to help with the large garden that had a lawn surrounded by flowers, and beyond was a shrubbery and a kitchen garden, full of fruit and vegetables.

Of course sugar was rationed, but the Captain had friends in the Caribbean and every so often they used to send over a very welcome supply. The kitchen was huge, and between the kitchen and the dining room was a long corridor, which was freezing cold and lined with lots of shelves. I used to fill all those shelves with jars of pickles and jams that I'd made. I worked there for five years and did learn how to cook!

There were one or two quite interesting characters that visited the house; one was General Smythe. He was a real Victorian figure, very military in his bearing, and I particularly remember his funeral. It was a very simple affair; his coffin was covered by a Union Flag and carried on a gun carriage drawn by horses. On top of the coffin sat his plumed helmet and sword. The mourners walked behind the gun carriage – very impressive.

Frances Fisher

We had a lovely house in Sycamore Road when we first came to Houghton Regis in the early 1960s. It had big windows, electricity, our own garden, it was really nice, I loved it; a whole new world and we lived there for a long time before we moved to Dunstable.

In London we lived in a semi-basement that had no electricity, so we had to use gaslights. We were only supposed to live there for ten months but ended up living there for ten years! It wasn't very nice, but we were a happy little family and I was so grateful to have a place to live that would take a child. When we found this basement, the landlady asked me if my baby was a boy, and when I said yes, she said, "I don't like boys." But she agreed to give us a 'try' and we moved in. I remember telling my husband I thought we'd only be there for a short time…

We lived in three rooms, a biggish front room, our bedroom and a living room. There was an old fashioned wash house, with an old copper in the corner which I never used, but if you did, you needed to fill it with paper, wood and coal to boil up the water. There was a garden that I shared with the owner, the lady that lived upstairs, but I wasn't even allowed to hang washing out. I loved living in London but with two children it was very crowded in our small flat, and we couldn't find anywhere else to live. We used to walk round the streets looking for a new flat. Sometimes we'd knock on the door of a house and ask if the owner had some empty rooms. But then we were always asked if we had a baby, and when we replied that yes we did, the response was the same - they didn't want any children in their house. It really was terrible and very hard to spend ten years living in that semi-basement with gaslight!

We had no television or record player because we had no electricity. We had an accumulator radio that we had to take round to the shop and get charged up every week. I used to listen to a programme called Jamaica Inn; I would rush home from wherever I was to listen to the next instalment. We lived near Finsbury Park and I'd take my children there.

Sometimes we'd get the bus and go to Alexandra Palace to ice skate

After almost ten years, my husband went to the employment exchange and found that jobs for men were available in Luton. It meant that he would need to travel into Luton every day, but after nine months we would be allocated a council house. He chose to work at Jackson's Cookers, and that's how we came to live in Houghton Regis. I was so delighted when he came home with this piece of paper, telling us that we had a house in Sycamore Road – I couldn't believe it!

I used to work as a school dinner lady in London and shortly after moving here I got a job as a dinner lady in Tithe Farm School, which I really enjoyed. When we moved here, the roads were built but the pathways were just gravel. There were no streetlights either, so it was all very basic, but they gradually built the pavements, put the lights in and finished building the schools. Although many houses had been built, there was still a lot of building work going on.

My children really liked the house, it was modern and new and they made lots of new friends playing on the Rec. But many people who came to live here from London were quite homesick, and wanted to go back because it was so different. I wasn't – I was glad to get out of that old basement! I think people soon got used to it and were quite happy. I soon made friends because everyone helped each other. People in the shops in the village weren't very fond of us initially. I think it was because we were sort of outsiders to them, but once they got to know us, we made friends.

William Aries

I was Church Warden, Verger and Sacristan at All Saints Church from 2006 to 2008. This means looking after and preparing the church and its contents for festivals and services, making sure the communion wine is available and helping to train the servers. I take care of just the sacristan side of the church now – it's quite interesting really.

We came to live in the town in the early seventies and helped to start the church in Parkside. We hadn't been here long when a young priest was sent to try and get what was known as St Thomas's Church going. The priest needed help, I agreed, and ended up being one of the youngest church wardens at the time.

A New Life...

Until St Thomas's was built, we met in the house of Rev Christopher Samuels in Enfield Close on Parkside. The Bishop of St Albans, the Rev Robert Runcie, consecrated it. It was unique, because it was made into a little local church for the community there.

We used to hold services in the house and then, when the congregation got bigger, we held services in Linmear School. I used to play a piano as well. It was a sort of do-it-yourself job! We did what we could, and they were good days. We started saving towards a proper building, and eventually St Thomas's Meeting House was built. After a time, it was decided to merge the two churches together, but the Meeting House is still there.

The Rev Derek Milton, Rev Chris Wood & Rev Geoffrey Neal (Vicar of Houghton Regis) at the opening of St Thomas's Meeting House in June 1988 (DG)

I can remember the Parkside Estate being developed and seeing the Barrett helicopter visiting and landing in the town. Back then Barrett Homes used a helicopter in their television advertisements, and on this one occasion they visited and actually landed the helicopter here, in Houghton Regis. My son and myself went to watch it. Luton Town Captain Paul Price came along to officially open the Barrett Estate - a big event in those days!

All Saints Church is very busy and very well supported. Many people spend a lot of time trying to raise money to keep the church in good order. The church is a listed building, and as you can imagine the restoration fund is never ending. The Tower was renovated a few years ago, and the bells were all restored again. They should see us all out!

Catherine Phillips, & Gloria Curruthers (nee Rowe)

We moved to the village in September 1959 from Aveley in Essex, when I was nine years old. Dad got a job at Vauxhall and had to commute to and from Aveley, going to work on Monday and coming home on Friday, until we were given the house in Peel Street.

Our parents were very happy to move to Houghton Regis. We visited the village during the summer to look around, and were chosen to have our pictures taken outside the house that we were allocated. Peel Street was one of the first roads to be lived in and we thought it was a really friendly place.

What a great opportunity to get a house, especially in those days. We were the first to move into our street and it was lovely with lots of places to go and play, especially the Tithe Farm and barns. We had plenty of fun playing there. Family and friends came to visit us a lot, of course.

Mr & Mrs Neal owned a smallholding at the side of our house; they were a very nice couple. They had an orchard and planted all sorts of vegetables and kept chickens and ducks. There are now six houses on that site. We used to buy our vegetables and eggs from them and they'd let us see the chicks hatching in the incubator. Sometimes we went down to the farm on Bidwell Hill to do pea and potato picking - what a backbreaking job that was! I belonged to the Girl Guilds and occasionally we'd help do the shopping for people living in the Alms Houses in front of All Saints Church.

A New Life...

Our dad kept the garden really nice and we were always playing there, front or back. We were taken to Beecroft School on coaches; many of the locals didn't like us but, never mind, and from there we went to Northfields. The school wasn't big enough when we first arrived, so they erected outbuildings that we used to call cowsheds! I enjoyed all my sports. I played netball for the school and ended up running for South Beds as well.

Catherine and Gloria in their garden in Peel Street (GC)

Mike Holwill

I was born in 1929 in Dulwich, East London and then moved with my parents to Kent when I was four years old. My father was employed by a textile importer in London that moved its offices to Heath & Reach after the war started. Most of my father's income came from bonuses, but the company imported from Germany, Japan and Czechoslovakia, all the places where frankly, during the war, there wasn't going to be much business conducted.

Times must have been quite hard - my father had to commute between Heath & Reach and Kent, but one of the people that he worked with had a house in Welwyn Garden City, and we sort of evacuated ourselves there. This made the commute rather less strenuous and soon after, he found a job working at Vauxhall Motors, and that's really how we came to live in this area.

We lived in Browning Road, and I too worked at Vauxhall's as an apprentice. I then served with the RAF while completing my national service. Prior to that, I had been courting a young lady in Houghton Regis who I subsequently married. Her mother and father lived in a row of cottages owned by her elderly aunt, just by the Five Bells Pub. We moved into one of those cottages when it became vacant after we married in 1952. Not long after moving in, one of the first things I was told I needed was an allotment. The garden at the cottage was virtually non-existent, so we went to see the vicar, paid our money and started growing vegetables!

The vicar was also on the parish council and 'volunteered' me to serve on there as well! I didn't mind, because I'd always believed in giving something back to society. After three or four years, though, because the council was politically motivated and I didn't want to be told to follow the party line, I gave it up. But while I was there, I represented the parish council on the Memorial Hall committee on a non-political basis, and I'm still a member of the committee today. It was an interesting time; the council was made up of people from all over the country and represented how the village has grown up.

The village had many characters; one of them was the gravedigger, Lol Bright. He walked with a definite twist and limp, which my old father-in-law told me he wasn't born with, he limped because that's the way his father walked, and he copied him. It is true or possible, I don't know? In my first courting days around the end of the war, when there was still a virtual blackout, I would walk my girlfriend home and then on the way home myself, past the church, I would suddenly hear a noise… it was Lol, digging a grave. He only ever dug graves at night, never during the day, and I think he lacked company, so he would stand and talk to whoever was passing. On numerous occasions at one o'clock in the morning I would be standing outside the church yard having a conversation with Lol!

Lol was also the caretaker at the Memorial Hall. The original hall was built where the car park now stands, and during the First World War

A New Life...

it was used as a canteen for the troops billeted on the Village Green.

During the war, as with most local communities, people from the village decided that a forces comfort fund should be set up. It was the done thing – you would send the troops cigarettes, gloves or a scarf; all the things you thought might help the lads at the front. At the end of the war there was still a substantial amount of money left in the fund, so a meeting was organised to decide what to do with it, and to choose a memorial. A decision was made to have something functional, and that's how the hall concept was started. The constitution of the hall was initially set up to represent the whole village, and representatives from various organisations were asked to form the committee. I was chairman of this committee for a long time, until I felt they needed someone younger to be involved and take over the chair.

Other fundraising for the hall also took place. In the early days we used to run a gymkhana every year. Col. Part allowed us to use the hall grounds for the gymkhana, and we had a huge turnout with people arriving from all over the country. We also held fetes on the Green, but the big event in those days was the beer barrel relay race which started up at the Five Bells pub and finished at the Green. The local pubs were invited to submit teams and it was quite an event - the police were very cooperative and used to close the road for us. But what I liked in those days, when we ran the fetes on the Green, you could turn to virtually anyone in the village and they would come along and help.

Gymkhana and Horse Show at Houghton Hall, 1949 (DG/LM)

Memories of Houghton Regis

Houghton Regis Fete, 1953 (DG/LM)

A New Life...

Richard Hall

We moved here in November 1965 from Tottenham, not long after we got married. I worked for London Transport as a vehicle fitter and had a flat in Muswell Hill. We married in March, but I was only earning about £9 per week, and we couldn't really afford to live there, as my wages only just covered our rent and rates. My wife was only paid around £2 a week working at Woolies, and it got to the stage where I'd have to go to work without any lunch. Eventually, my foreman contacted the welfare department, and we were asked if we would like to move out into an expanding town like Hemel, Stevenage, Hitchin or Luton, where there were also country garages.

We agreed, and they arranged it all. Luton Rural District Council found us a house in the village. At first I travelled between Muswell Hill and Luton from May until the 13th November, when we eventually moved.

We lived in Vicarage Road for eleven years, until we bought our own house in Drury Lane. We loved it here - not like the push and shove of London, and ideal for children.

I am very interested in local history and, knowing this, Mrs Neal who lived in a cottage near to our house, gave me a copy of a sales brochure from agents selling properties in the village in 1913. The sale was held in the Sugar Loaf Hotel, Dunstable. The cottage Mrs Neal lived in (according to the brochure) was used as a laundry, and, including land and an orchard, was sold for £71. Other properties and land in Houghton Regis were advertised for sale, including Thorn Farm sold for £1,420, and three cottages at the bottom of Dury Lane sold for £400.

Irene Carpenter

I was born in St John's Wood in London in 1937, in my grandmother's house and slept in a drawer!

I married in 1958 and moved here in 1963, after living with my parents and then with my husband's parents for five years, while we saved up for a deposit on a house. Back then you had to have quite a good deposit; they didn't take the woman's salary into consideration and as fast as we were saving, the prices of houses were rising. So we decided to look

By Direction of Messrs. REDHEAD & GRAY, *Ltd.*

BEDFORDSHIRE.

Important Sale of a Portion of the

Houghton Regis & Dunstable Estates

Particulars, with Plans and Conditions of Sale of

Small Holdings. :: :: Cottages. Accommodation and Building Land.

COMPRISING

THORN FARM

with Homestead and about 45 Acres, let to Mr. J. FENSOM on a Michaelmas tenancy.

3 EXCELLENT ENCLOSURES OF MEADOW LAND between Calcutt and Thorn Farms, let to Mr. TURNER on a Michaelmas tenancy.

AT WINGFIELD. Orchard, 2 Meadows and 22 Acres of Fertile Arable Land, let to Mr. WHINNETT on a Michaelmas tenancy.

AT BIDWELL. A valuable parcel of Accommodation Land, about 2½ Acres.

AT HOUGHTON REGIS. Valuable Meadow, 2 Acres, 2 Roods, 23 Poles, at East End. A piece of well stocked Kitchen Ground adjoining.

2 Capital enclosures of Accommodation Land, 5 Acres, 2 Roods, 0 Poles, on the Sundon Road.

Brick built and thatched double-fronted Cottage with about Half-an-Acre of Garden in Luton Road.

Cottage, Outbuildings and Orchard in Drury Lane, adjoining Tithe Farm, let to Mrs. HUDSON.

Nos. 1, 2, 3, Park Cottages, The Green, all let to good Tenants.

5 Acres of Accommodation or Building Land with about 150 feet frontage to Mixt Way.

AT CHALK HILL. Brick built Cottage and Land, let to Miss LINNEY, having a frontage to Watling Street of about 80 feet.

MESSRS. NORBURY, SMITH & CO.

Have received instructions to offer the above by Auction in Lots (*unless previously disposed of by private treaty*)

On WEDNESDAY, the 17th day of September, 1913,

At SIX p.m. precisely,

AT THE "SUGAR LOAF" HOTEL, DUNSTABLE.

Particulars, Plans and Conditions of Sale may be had from Messrs. CLIFFORD TURNER & HOPTON, Solicitors, 80, Finsbury Pavement, E.C.; Messrs. BENNING & SON, Solicitors, Dunstable; or of the Auctioneers, at their Offices, 23, High Street North, Dunstable, or

Telephone—Gerrard 7872; and Dunstable 47.   5, GEORGE STREET, HANOVER SQUARE, LONDON, W

Copy of sales brochure listing properties in Houghton Regis and Dunstable, 1913 (RH)

A New Life...

outside of London. We came to have a look at the village during the winter after it had been snowing. The estate agent told us that this little area was called Little Siberia, because it got so cold! We put a deposit down straightaway. We could afford it, we'd been married five years and we wanted a family. We were in heaven; they were such lovely houses, with part central heating - unheard of then!

We were one of the last people to move into our road, and everyone around us were our sort of age. Many people had come from London and some were local. Immediately we all made friends. Everyone would help each other and we had great parties. We'd all bring round a plate of food to someone's house and then the next day, we'd go round and help clear up. Back then everyone seemed to be living with grandma's old sofa and nothing on the floor, and it took a time before we could all save up and buy new furniture and carpets. It was wonderful – I'd felt like I'd moved into a little village in the middle of the countryside, surrounded by beautiful fields and hills. There wasn't much here, just a few little shops and I was quite shocked when I walked into Perry's - it had sawdust on the floor!

In 1968, when my son was two, I joined the local Women's Institute. That branch had been going strong since 1945 and when I joined they had about seventy members. It was very formal, they wore hats and everyone called everyone else by their surname, Mrs ...so and so. After I had been there ten years, I became the secretary, and I still am! However, we've only got sixteen members now. It works quite well really - we're all friends and go out together. I don't think so many women are as interested in joining today, and as we're all getting older, I don't think we would cope with many more members.

I've loved living here, I've never regretted moving – London is all right, but Houghton has a village feel about it. I got to know a number of the original people from the village, through joining the WI. They weren't very happy when Tithe Farm Estate was built. You can imagine, there was this lovely little village and then suddenly they built this big estate. But a number of women from Tithe Farm came and joined our branch and they were so thrilled with their houses. They'd been living in the slums of London; some of them had been bombed out, perhaps two or three times during the war, and it was heaven to them.

Memories of Houghton Regis

Houghton Regis WI Bazaar, 1953 (DG/LM)

A New Life...

Houghton Regis WI celebrates its 60th anniversary in the Memorial Hall (DG)
Back row: l to r: Marian Hill, Theresa Pritchett, Marian Saper
Middle row: Shirley Skuce, Margaret Robinson, Marilyn Woodley, Betty Moret, Joyce Denny, May Falrey, Sally Longford
Front row: Sandra Barrat, Beverly Lennox, Jean Cheshire, Irene Carpenter

Memories of Houghton Regis

Members of the Houghton Regis Women's Institute in 1954 (DG)

Chris Charman

I lived next to a famous landmark, because I lived next door to what we called the 'Pink House'. The house had been rendered and painted bright pink, so when you came up Tithe Farm Hill, it was the first thing you'd see. A lot of people called it Hansel & Gretel's Cottage, because it had brown shutters and ornaments in the garden.

My parents were Londoners and shared a townhouse there, but it was very expensive. My dad found a job at Skefco's and commuted for six months on a moped, staying in digs above a café before they were allocated a house in Hillbrough Crescent. I was born in that house in 1963. They said they were so glad to have their own front door, and a bath – in London they'd had to use a tin bath in front of the fire. That bath came with them from London and became a fish pond in our garden.

I think my parents missed London. My mum took some time to settle here, but she was at home bringing up myself and my two older brothers, and felt a bit isolated. They'd left their roots behind but they lived alongside a lot of other newcomers and made many friends. It was also a time when everyone left their doors unlocked because it was safe to do so, and no-one had anything worth stealing anyway. There was none of this "keeping up with the Jones' ", everyone was just glad to have a roof over their heads. My grandfather followed us by moving here in 1968, following his retirement from Twining's Tea factory, after he'd worked there for forty-nine years.

I've noticed a lot of changes throughout the time I've lived here. As a child, a big treat on a Sunday was the arrival of the fish van where we'd buy a pint of prawns, and being Londoners all the family liked their cockles, winkles and prawns. A paraffin van would visit the estate selling fuel for heaters and the Corona lorry came round regularly. We used to buy six bottles of fizzy drink and get excited because we could keep the money that we got from returning the empty bottles.

We had lots of freedom and space to explore. We'd pack sandwiches and stay out all day. We used to go and play in Spooky Woods! It was at the top end of the estate – we'd cross fields and a small stream and play there. I also used to cycle a lot around the town. They started to build the Parkside estate in the early 1970s, and I hated Parkside, I didn't want it to be built. They constructed it in stages and I used to cycle around the

Memories of Houghton Regis

estate and ring my bell to annoy people – they'd taken over the fields we used to play on. Lo and behold, I now live here myself...

Michael Heseltine, Under Secretary of State for the Environment, visiting one of the new houses on Parkside Estate 1971 (DG/LM)

Mr D R Riley

Leafing through a newspaper one day I came across an article about new towns that were being built after the war. Houghton Regis just happened to be one of them. I visited a couple of places, but when I came to see the village, I just fell for it - I really liked the place.

To get a house in London, you had to wait years, but if you moved out of the city, into one of the new or expanding towns you could get a house within eight weeks. Officials came to see you in your own home in London, to make sure it was kept in good order before you were allocated a house elsewhere! My wife couldn't wait to leave London; she had a terrible cough brought on by the smog in the city every winter.

At that time I was working at Sainsbury's in Earl's Court in London, and I requested a transfer to the Luton branch in George Street. I slept over the shop for eight weeks in accommodation for staff to stay overnight. After the eight weeks, we came to see this house - it was a re-let and we decided to take it. Lots of people did the same sort of thing. They got jobs, many at Vauxhall, and stayed in digs until they were entitled to a council house.

We eventually moved here in 1963 from Lambeth in London. It was a beautiful village with lots of little shops in the High Street, Workhouse Row in front of the church and the Tithe Barn further along the road. There was a general store opposite the church; it reminded me of a Wild West saloon, because it had swing doors.

Most of our estate was built then, but we heard tales from the pioneers that came here before us, of roads and pavements unfinished, having to walk miles to a bus stop and mud everywhere!

We were so happy to live in the village, we never regretted moving here. It was very easy to make friends because everyone was in the same boat - lots of people had moved away from friends and family for a new life in Houghton Regis.

Memories of Houghton Regis

Houghton Regis aerial view c 1968 (DG/LM)

ROYAL HOUGHTON
The Story of Houghton Regis Bedfordshire
Pat Lovering

People still find parish churches a fascination, so that week by week visitors to our church for weddings and baptisms especially stop to ask questions. How old is the church? Where did Regis come from? These and many other questions are the beginning of the fascinating trail taking us back nearly one thousand years.

Did you know that Houghton Regis was a Royal Manor in Saxon times? It also appeared in the Doomsday Book of 1086. Henry 1st gave land from his manor of Houghton Regis to make the new town of Dunstable.

All these facts and many other details of Houghton Regis from earliest times to present day are included in this book.

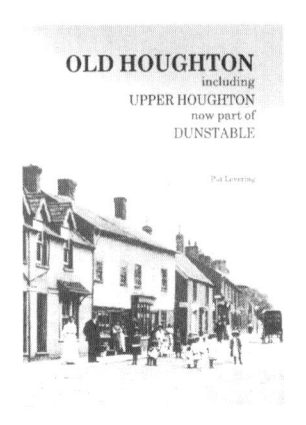

OLD HOUGHTON
including Upper Houghton now part of Dunstable
Pat Lovering

More than 170 photographs of village life in historic Houghton Regis, Bedfordshire, taken over the last 100 years and acquired from both private and public sources are included in this publication. Because of subsequent boundary changes many early photographs cover parts of modern Dunstable.

The author Pat Lovering, is a local private tutor who has lived and worked in Houghton Regis and Dunstable for some years. She became interested in assembling this collection of photographs when compiling her other book "Royal Houghton".

FROM COUNTRY BOY TO WEATHERMAN
A Houghton and Dunstable Youth
George Jackson

A memoir of the author's childhood and teenage years growing up in the village of Houghton Regis. It covers his earliest pre-school memories, his time at primary school in the village and then at Dunstable Grammar School. He remembers family and village life in the immediate post-war years with fondness and humour.
He also takes a mental stroll around the village, as he knew it, stopping off along the way to describe some of the buildings and other features and many of the characters associated with them. It is perhaps not a picture of any particular year but rather an amalgam of memories of a period of around twelve years up to when everything began to change dramatically with the development of the Tithe Farm Estate.
Later the author remembers his first job employed in different departments of the Meteorological Office at Dunstable including working on Meteor, one of the first computers in the country, and a brief period when he was still living in Houghton Regis but working at an operational RAF station at Bovingdon in Hertfordshire. Sporting and motorcycling exploits and a fairly hectic social life in Dunstable and surrounding area are not neglected.

DUNSTABLE AND DISTRICT AT WAR
FROM EYE WITNESS ACCOUNTS
Compiled by Jean Yates and Sue King

Dunstable and District at War is mainly a collection of personal reminiscences, by people who lived here or who called Dunstable home during the Second World War. Hundreds of recent interviews have recaptured these unique memories that evoke the disrupted, day-to-day life of an archetypal rural town in that unique period of British history.

Bedfordshire was at the heart of the Secret War and Dunstable was very much a part of it. The Meteorological Office was based at the bottom of the Downs, and forecasters worked closely with Bomber Command to decide the date for D-Day.

This book tries to give a feel for where Dunstable sat in the wider picture; the relationships it had and the part it played in conjunction with Bletchley Park, Black Propaganda, SOE and our Allies.

A final chapter recounts a few of the remarkable contributions Dunstablians made to the various battlefronts overseas, including D-Day and the Far East.

Enclosed with this book is an audio disc containing snippets of some of the recollections. The compilers hope you enjoy reading and listening to these extraordinary stories as much as they have.

Book Castle PUBLISHING

STRAW HATS AND BONNETS
Joan Curran

Straw Hats and Bonnets is not a history of the cottage industry of straw plaiting, but the story of Dunstable hat manufacturers of the 19th century, when hats were made in factories and the industry was the mainstay of the economy of the town. It begins in the late 18th century and ends in the early 20th. Over those years there were many hat factories in Dunstable, ranging from small family concerns to large firms employing three to four hundred people.

The first part of the book is a general history of the industry from 1785 to 1931, when the last factory closed. The second part is in the form of a hat trail, in which you will find the individual stories of the thirteen major firms who were manufacturing hats when the trade was at its peak, in the 1870s and the early 1880s.

DUNSTABLE DOWN THE AGES
An outline history from prehistoric to modern times
Joan Schneider and Vivienne Evans

People have lived in South Bedfordshire for thousands of years, even before the Roman constructed Watling Street, and a town grew up where Dunstable now stands on the crossing with the Icknield Way.

Then came Anglo Saxon immigrants, and the creation of a new town and a Priory by Henry 1st. There was a royal residence, and a Queen Eleanor Cross was built, after her coffin rested at the Priory. The decision which ended Henry VIII's first marriage and caused England's break with the Roman Catholic Church, was taken here. The following century saw religious controversy causing violent clashes in Dunstable.

Almshouses and schools were founded on the proceeds of distilling gin. Long distance coaches appeared on improved roads, and inns for travellers, but there were highwaymen too. Straw bonnets sold to the travellers started the hat trade, which flourished in Victorian times.

EXPLORING HISTORY ALL AROUND
Vivienne Evans

A handbook of local history, arranged as a series of routes to cover Bedfordshire and adjoining parts of Hertfordshire and Buckinghamshire. It is organised as two books in one. There are seven thematic sections full of fascinating historical detail and anecdotes for armchair reading. Also it is a perfect source of family days out as the book is organised as circular motoring/cycling explorations, highlighting attractions and landmarks. Also included is a background history to all the major towns in the area, plus dozens of villages, which will enhance your appreciation and understanding of the history that is all around you!

KING OF 'THE CALI'
A Lifetime in Rock 'n Roll
Russ Sainty

The legendary 'Cali' venue on Dunstable Downs, Bedfordshire was a magnet for almost every top rock and pop act of the sixties – Tom Jones, The Hollies, The Bee Gees, The Walker Brothers, The Rolling Stones, The Searchers, Craig Douglas, Brian Poole and The Tremeloes, The Barron Knights, P.J. Proby, The Dave Clark Five, The Tornados, Lulu, The Eagles, The Byrds, Billy Fury, Dusty Springfield, The Who, Stevie Wonder...the list goes on and on.

But one performer above all was synonymous with The Cali, performing no less than an incredible 336 sessions up to the mid-sixties, including the magical opening night of March 12th 1960. Now that star, Russ Sainty, takes us behind the scenes to share some of his 'Cali Happenings'.

Russ's story is a roller-coaster ride of triumph and disappointment, but he tells it all with truth and integrity. Life has always been fun and never predictable for the King of the Cali.

THE CALI ALBUM
Life and Times at
The California Ballroom, Dunstable
Diane Ilka

Hundreds of the now iconic pop stars of the sixties and seventies performed live at the unique California Ballroom in Dunstable.

Diane Ilka - granddaughter of the 'Cali's' founder - lived and worked there. A generation on, she has compiled a tribute to this very special phenomenon in pop music's history, including many pictures and contract details from her private collection of memorabilia. All those who were part of the 'Cali' era can now reminisce over the stars and dates that formed a highlight of their most impressionable years.

Book Castle
PUBLISHING